Louis and Fanny

LOUIS AND FANNY

DAN PEDERSEN

Louis and Fanny

15 Years on the Alaska Frontier

DAN PEDERSEN

LOUIS AND FANNY

Copyright © 2017 Dan Pedersen

All rights reserved.

ISBN: 1541113918
ISBN-13: 978-1541113916

DAN PEDERSEN

DEDICATION

For all the Pedersens and Turners.

*

We are each one of us a bundle of his ancestors. Been reading about all those ribbons of DNA, literally billions of miles of them in each one of us, coiling back through the generations. We are what our ancestors have made of us, virtues and vices, warts, sins and all. – The Voyage, by Philip Caputo

CONTENTS

Prologue: A Century Afterwards		9
Family Tree – Simplified		13

*

1	Preparing to Die		14
	Aboard the *USRC Manning*		
	Aboard the *Dora*		
2	Four Mounds of Snow		22
3	An Inseparable Team		28
	Louis and Fanny		
	Fanny's Father, Joseph		
	John Wesley Turner, Fanny's Uncle		
	Fanny's World		
4	The Tent		38
	Moving Into the Parsonage		
5	The Parson's Picture Show		44
6	Following the Rails		48
	1909-1910: The Triumphant Trip Outside		
	Guests of a New York City Financier		
	Paradise on the Hudson		
7	Playing With Bears		57
	The Preacher's Darkroom		
	An Alaskan Joins the Family		
8	'Louie, Our House is on Fire'		65
9	The Ivory Napkin Ring		68
10	The Family Glacier		70
11	End of the Beginning		74

12	War on Saloons	78
	Louis's Switch from Methodist to Presbyterian	
	Pedersen Brothers Photography	
	Ralph Edits *The Skagway Daily Alaskan*	
	Joe Runs Away to Seattle	
	Louis Travels Outside for His Mother	
	Tuberculosis	
13	The Sophia Disaster	94
14	Fanny's Death	97

*

Epilogue: 'Be Useful'	101
Appendix 1: The L.H. Pedersen Family	104
Appendix 2: Joe Pedersen Interview	116
Appendix 3: Willard Pedersen Interview	134
Appendix 4: Ruth Pedersen Interview	130
Appendix 5: Pedersens in Wrangell	182
Appendix 6: Pedersens in Skagway	183
Acknowledgments	202
About the Author	205

LOUIS AND FANNY

PROLOGUE – A CENTURY AFTERWARDS

"You folks visiting?" the Seward cabbie asked. It was a good guess. My wife Sue and I had just stepped off the Alaska Ferry and clambered into the waiting cab. The woman seemed jumpy, like she'd taken some pills.

"Looking around," I said. "My grandparents lived here a century ago."

"Really? Who were they?"

"Louis and Fanny Pedersen."

"Seriously?" she asked. Suddenly her eyes were on us – in the rearview mirror.

"*You're* related to Louie Pedersen?" (Holy cow. I thought only Louis's wife called him that.)

"You know of him?"

"*Everyone* knows of him."

Then gravity pressed us into our seats as this wild woman sped through the streets – drunk or high or something – me wondering

LOUIS AND FANNY

how she had ever heard of my grandparents.

We arrived on the *MV Kennicott* from Juneau on a sunny July morning of 2000. Our journey across the Gulf of Alaska retraced the route of Louis and Fanny Pedersen's ship, the *SS Portland*, 95 years earlier that month. They stepped ashore July 31, 1905, to a barely civilized landscape in this same place.

Louis Klaus Olaus Haapstock Pedersen and Mary Frances Turner Pedersen went north as Methodist missionaries to change the world. By the time they returned they'd left their name on Pedersen Glacier. It was the most visible mark they made on the map but the least of their marks on Alaska.

This account of their 15-year adventure owes a profound debt to my sister-in-law Lisa Pedersen for some priceless audio interviews she recorded in the 1970s.

Lisa, my brother Fred's second wife, was new to the family, and to the West Coast and her new hometown of Tacoma. She enrolled in a history class that called for original research, and knew that her new family had a rich and colorful heritage.

Lisa interviewed at length three of Louis and Fanny's seven children – Ruth, Willard and my dad, Joe – all now deceased. That entire generation has passed and there will be no more chances to ask them questions that could help us better understand who they were, and who *we* are.

In the 1990s I obtained Lisa's brittle cassette tapes and set about transcribing them – tedious work. Portions were indecipherable, but with effort I retrieved most of the words. My grandparents came alive in these transcripts – eyewitness accounts of the adventure they lived in turn-of-the-century Alaska, spoken in their own children's words.

Each of the three children contributed different memories. Together, their recollections shape a surprisingly complete account.

Most readers, like me, probably translate the word "Appendix" to mean, "Don't read this." But Lisa's interviews in Appendices 2, 3 and 4 of this book are highly informative, worthwhile and entertaining reading.

I owe immense gratitude to my Uncle Willard, who worked with me on this project after most of his siblings were gone. He embraced technology and collaborated by email into the last years of his life, feeding me scarce family photographs and leads for this work. He was 96 when he died in 2007.

Children in large families are born at different times and grow up with different memories. To be a preacher's kid adds pressures and expectations. Willard's memories as the youngest child in the household (for a time) were dramatically different from my dad's. My dad was 12 years older and had 12 more years to know his mother, whom he adored, before she died at age 49. Those were 12 more years to get into some testy conflicts with his dad.

Willard was just nine when his mom died in routine surgery. His dad seemed cold and aloof. "To tell the truth I hardly knew him," Willard once snapped with an uncharacteristic edge in his voice. Later he wept when we found a poem his dad had written about his mother's untimely death.

Willard shared with me the raw excitement of discovery. I miss him terribly. Together, we pieced together Louis and Fanny's story, and back-story, which led in directions neither of us foresaw.

I never met my grandparents. Fanny died in 1920 and Louis in 1939, long before I was born in 1947. But Louis left hundreds of breadcrumbs revealing where he traveled, and with whom, thanks to a technological revolution in 1907.

That is the year Kodak introduced its "real photo post card," enabling hobbyists like Louis to transfer any image they took to a post card they could send or sell to others. A half-decent photographer in Alaska could do well selling post cards to tourists. The trail of post cards Louis created now is part of the photographic archive of early Alaska history.

Half of this book consists of appendices. They add a wealth of details about the family and community life on Alaska's frontier a century ago. They are well worth reading – a look back in time as source documents never before published.

Louis & Fanny's Parents and Children

Fanny's parents
Joseph H. Turner 1843-1905
Martha Brownfield 1848-1940

Louis's parents
Klaus Olaus Pedersen Lokanut 1835-1867
Maren Anna Groven 1849-1926

Louis and Fanny had six children. Following Fanny's death in 1920, Louis married Ada Marion Holt in 1921 and she took over as mother to Fanny's large family. Marion and Louis together brought a seventh child into the family, Dorothy.

Rev. Louis H. Pedersen 1867-1939
Mary Frances Turner 1870-1920

> **Rev. Frederick L. Pedersen** 1893-1976 m. Ethel LaViolette
> *No children*
> **Ralph M. Pedersen** 1894-1976 m. Gertrude May Foote
> > **Richard** F. Pedersen m. Nelda Newell Napier
> > Rev. **Ralph** M. Pedersen Jr. m. Marilyn M. Strahl
> **Joe Turner Pedersen** 1899-1992 m. Mildred I. Pederson
> > **Fred** Pedersen m. Elizabeth (Lisa) Ann Larsen
> > **Joe** Finrow Pedersen m. Sharon Grace Vermillion
> > **Frances** Elizabeth Pedersen
> > **Dan** Pedersen m. Suzanne Brelsford, later remarried Sue Van Etten
> **Ruth Frances Pedersen Haugen** 1902-1987
> *Brief marriage. No children*
> **Willard S. Pedersen** 1911-2007 m. Helen Clark Hunter
> > **Douglas** Hunter Pedersen m. Janice Mortlock
> **Andrew Groven Pedersen** 1916-2003 m. Elsie M. Wallis
> > **Nancy** Ruth Pedersen m. Jerry M. Leavitt
> > **Andrew** James Pedersen m. Judith Gay Knowles

Ada Marion Holt 1880-1971

> **Dorothy M. Pedersen Vogel** 1922-2012 m. Owen A. Vogel
> > **Janis** Vogel m. Pat Collins
> > **Judith** Vogel m. Michael Chesney

Chapter 1

Preparing to Die

Trees sagged under a blanket of white. Boots kicked up powder in the streets of Seward, Alaska, as the mail steamer *Dora* pulled away from the dock. The ship trailed a plume of black smoke. Captain C.B McMullen stood at the stern, taking a last look at civilization and pondering what he'd find on his return to Kodiak.

He'd just reached Seward with a firsthand account of conditions in the remote outpost of Kodiak. Mt. Katmai had exploded 100 miles from Kodiak in a volcanic eruption that was still spewing ash into the atmosphere. The *Dora* had called on Kodiak after tense hours sailing blind in conditions that could have cost McMullen the ship and all aboard.

Now he was going back with the minister's wife. The Aleutians were part of the regular circuit of his 112-foot steam-and-sail vessel, with 16 staterooms and a crew of 20.

At the rail amidships, next to the lifeboat, Fanny Pedersen in white waved to her husband, Louis, who waved back and snapped one last photograph.

Louis and Fanny Pedersen were Methodist missionaries to Alaska. They had arrived in Seward just a few years earlier.

The preacher's wife was likely the only passenger on this outbound leg, and likely the only woman. She and Capt. McMullen were the

The *Dora* leaves Seward with Fanny at the rail amidships and Captain McMullen at the stern. *Louis Pedersen photo*

only people on deck.

Fanny had weighed this decision, calculating the risk. She and Louis trusted the captain, a man of culture and experience, a family friend and sometime guest in their home. In fact two years later McMullen brought Louis an ivory napkin ring from Dutch Harbor for him to give Fanny as an anniversary gift. The ring now resides in the Seward museum.

McMullen's firsthand account of conditions in Kodiak convinced Fanny she must go. Also on board was another friend, mail clerk John Thwaites, a well-read man and avid photographer like Louis, and also a houseguest at times.

"We have no choice," Fanny told Louis. "We have to make sure those children are ok."

The children on her mind, mostly Aleut natives, lived in the Baptist orphanage on Woody Island, across from the settlement of Kodiak, and Fanny's determination to go went beyond charity. She and Louis had put four of those children in the Woody Island orphanage themselves, just a few years before. She could not turn her back on them.

But this trip meant leaving her husband and eight-month-old baby Willard after a very personal disaster – a winter-night fire that lit up the night in Seward as it consumed their own home.

The volcanic explosion of June 6, 1912 was catastrophic but came after some warnings. Earthquakes shook Seward for days leading up to it. Then on that June afternoon, 200 miles west of the Pedersen home, the largest explosion of the 20th Century blew the top off Mt. Katmai in the Kenai Peninsula.

It left a hole three miles wide, and everything that had been in that hole now boiled thousands of feet into the atmosphere, carried on superheated air, suspended over a vast area of Earth. When it came down it would make life miserable for all in its path. But that first explosion was only the beginning. Ten hours afterwards came the second, and 12 hours after that, the third.

On Kodiak Island, ash filled the sky and blacked out the town for 60 hours. Landslides of ash swept away houses. People went hungry and expected to die. Lightning struck the Naval radio station, setting it afire and knocking out communication with the outside world. Ships' radios were useless with the electrical disturbance. Townspeople waited in darkness, their eyes and throats burning with dust, wondering if they could survive this, whatever it was.

Downwind, ash rained for a day at Juneau, across the Gulf of Alaska. In Vancouver, B.C., more than 1,000 miles from the volcano, people wondered if the sulfuric atmosphere was safe to breathe. It all happened just as the *Dora* was returning from its westward run, bound for Kodiak, a few hours ahead. It waited offshore till conditions cleared enough to approach Kodiak, then continued on to Seward.

USRC Manning arrives in Seward with Kodiak refugees. *Louis Pedersen photo*

Aboard the US Revenue Cutter *Manning* . . .

The *Dora* was one of two ships battling the ash. The Revenue cutter *USRC Manning* was the other. It was in port at St. Paul on Kodiak Island when the eruption began, and was trapped there for a time.

Captain K.W. Perry feared the island might become buried in ash like the ancient city of Pompeii. He and his crew took townspeople aboard and provided eye care and other medical attention to the terrified population. Perry's detailed account is preserved in the *Annual Report of the US Revenue-Cutter Service*, for 1912.

"All streams and wells had now become choked," Perry reported, "and the advisability of the *Manning* getting to sea was discussed. However this was out of the question, as few of the inhabitants wished to leave, and the voice of the ship's company was, 'Take all or none.'" It's worth noting that, at this time, no one knew where the explosion had taken place, or what was coming next.

"Deep concern was visible on every countenance," Perry wrote. His ship's crew worked tirelessly to cope with the ash that coated everything.

"All hands were on duty from 7 a.m. Men often collided in working about decks, as the feeble glow of the electric lights and lanterns failed to dispel the awful darkness for any distance. The crew kept constantly at work with shovels, and four streams of water from the fire mains were playing incessantly in what at times seemed a vain effort to clear the ship of its horrible burden."

"I called together a committee meeting of the officers of the ship and several citizens, among whom were local pilots, and it was agreed that, as every landmark was obliterated, that it was impossible to see from the bridge, and that as the chances were vastly against a ship making the narrow channel without striking, it was better to stay where we were and take what most of us believed to be only a fighting chance."

The entire population assembled on the wharf, 149 in the warehouse and 185 aboard the *Manning*.

"Shortly before 11 a.m. Lieut. W.K. Thompson of the *Manning* informed me that several men were cut off in the cannery, about one half of a mile distant below our dock. He stated that he had a party willing to try a rescue and asked for orders. I replied that I would not give him orders, for it might be sending men to death, but that he and his party might have my permission to make an attempt."

The volunteers succeeded.

On June 8, Capt. Perry concluded it was possible to attempt departure, and that to stay where they were might mean death. With the townspeople aboard, the *Manning* successfully navigated the narrow channel to the outer harbor and sent a motorboat to Woody Island to bring off all 103 inhabitants. "Many were nearly famished for food and water," Perry reported, "while others demanded the attention of doctors and nurses. This day food and water were furnished to 486 people, outside our own crew.

By the morning of June 9, the sky had cleared and the *Manning* sent parties ashore on Kodiak and Woody islands to assess conditions.

"Having found that the people of Woody Island could with safety return to their homes, at 3:15 pm I sent all of them ashore except widows, children and the sick, who were un-provided for or needed medical aid.

The immediate crisis was past, but the effects would continue.

Louis and Fanny's son, Joe, later recalled, "For about two weeks we had earthquakes in Seward four, five, six times a day. Sometimes the dishes rattled and sometimes they fell from the shelves. Ash and smoke blotted out the sun for two weeks. Daylight was weird! Sometimes at night we could see great flashes of light and flames over the mountains to the southwest."

The *Dora* had almost made it to Kodiak on the evening of the eruption, before conditions became impossible. Mail clerk, Thwaites, wrote in his personal account, *In the Ashes of an Eruption:*

Aboard the *Dora*

"The day was an exceptionally beautiful one and we were all on deck enjoying our cigar and the scenery when someone shouted: 'Look at the smoke.' Gazing off to the westward we beheld across Shelikof Straits, on the mainland, an immense column of smoke ascending skyward, its diameter seeming to be at least half a mile or a mile."

The volcano was 55 miles from their position, and Thwaites went on, "Of course we all thought of our cameras, but the distance was so great that the idea of securing a photograph was abandoned as impractical. We continued to watch the phenomenon when it began to dawn upon our minds that it was rapidly becoming dimmer, and that a dark mass of cloud was showing above the column, mingling with it and coming our way."

"We watched the cloud with considerable interest," Thwaites said, "as it seemed different in some way, being especially black and forbidding. Presently, someone reported seeing a flash of lightening. We laughed at the statement, asking him where he thought he was, as lightning is practically unknown in this part of the world. But we did not laugh long."

Soon, lightning filled the sky. "The minute that cloud came between us and the sun, it began to grow strangely dark," Thwaites said.

Captain McMullen's worries at this point suddenly became intense. "All steam was crowded on in an effort to reach Kodiak before the ashes should completely envelope us."

They didn't make it. "The shower of ashes had increased until the beaches and cliffs along the neighboring shore showed white and ghastly through the deep gloom. The ship had threaded the last torturous channel before reaching the entrance of Kodiak Harbor, now but a few miles away, when the last ribbon of clear sky was obscured, the light snuffed out like a candle, and we were left in absolute darkness.

"We had to feel our way around the deck," Thwaites said. Ships officers closed all windows but still, ash seeped into the bridge. "It was with the greatest difficulty that the man at the wheel could see the ship's compass through the thick dust that filled the room."

McMullen sailed blind till he believed he was about three miles from his destination, then turned at right angles and broke for the open ocean. There the ship remained overnight in what Thwaites called inky blackness.

"During the night the wind had freshened until by morning it was blowing a living gale," Thwaites said. "The sea had assumed tremendous proportions but we did not mind that. Sweating, panting and exhausted, all who were not on duty rolled into our ash-laden beds and slept far into the day."

It was now June 7, and for the next 24 hours the *Dora* watched the column of smoke in the distance. Not till June 9 did the *Dora* approach Kodiak again, finding the landscape blanketed with ash, sand and pumice, in some places several feet deep.

Crops and gardens were buried, machinery jammed with ash, and communications knocked out. Residents struggled to see and breathe. But miraculously no one had died, and after stopping the *Dora* was able to continue on to Seward with its report, and pick up Fanny. By the time she reached Kodiak and Woody Island on the return voyage, the immediate crisis had passed. Life would go on.

But for Fanny and her husband, Louis, living on the edge of civilization in Seward, life was often complicated.

Louis and Fanny as newlyweds in 1890.

Chapter 2

Four Mounds of Snow With Four White Crosses

"Mrs. Pedersen, he yours. You take. He yours. This my Johnny – he yours."

Louis and Fanny's daughter Ruth remembers the day.

"One day my folks went down to the beach and found a tiny baby nursing a dead mother – a little black-eyed, black-haired boy two weeks old. The father, known locally as Billy Lowell, was of course grief stricken. He didn't know what to do with the baby."

Little Johnny was just one of five children Billy Lowell gave Louis and Fanny in 1906, a year after they arrived in Seward. After they accepted the baby, Billy gave them four more. It was beyond what they could do. Since arriving in Seward in 1905 they'd been living in a tent (more about this later) with four children of their own. Bringing five more children into the tent was out of the question. They sent the four oldest Lowell children to Woody Island.

" . . . My (parents) found a great need among the natives and half-breeds who lived on the beaches in rather disheveled conditions," Ruth said. "One family by the name of Lowell was in extremely poor circumstances. My folks tried to help them with clothing, food and fuel. The children were dirty, infested with vermin, and the mother was sick in bed, dying of tuberculosis. Their father was a half-breed related to the poet James Russell Lowell. His father was the brother of James Russell Lowell."

This brother had taken a common-law wife and these were their children.

"So my parents took the baby home and made plans to adopt him legally," Ruth said. "We all loved him – little Johnny, big black eyes – but he didn't have a chance. As I recall he lived about a year.

"Uh, after this baby died, there were four older children Billy Lowell wanted my folks to also adopt. That was more than they could manage, so Mother took them over to the Baptist orphanage on Woody Island, near Kodiak. They were in our home for several weeks while awaiting transportation to this orphanage."

Ruth said the children ranged from age 4 to about 12 or 13. "I recall being sent out of the house one day while some members of the Ladies Aid were deeply engrossed with these children. Something was going on and I was dying to know what, so I peeked through the window. They were going after these children's hair with little fine-tooth combs and coal oil."

LOUIS AND FANNY

Frank and Mary Lowell are said to have been the first Americans to live on Resurrection Bay, having settled there in the 1880s or 90s. Frank was a New Englander who purchased supplies from the Alaska Commercial Company and traded them to the natives in exchange for furs. Mary was of mixed race, part Russian and part native – Eskimo, Aleut or Knik.

Archaeologist Michael Yarborough believes Frank may have come to Resurrection Bay ahead of Mary to establish a saltery for preserving fish. Mary's homestead filing gives a date of August 1888. In any case, in 1893 Frank abandoned Mary and the nine children, who remained on the land. Effectively isolated, they carried on a successful subsistence lifestyle and built several homes and outbuildings.

When the Frank and John Ballaine party arrived seeking land for an ice-free seaport, Mary agreed to sell the developers all her land for $4,000 and several lots in the town. She and her children continued to live on the beach near the current site of the Alaska Sea-Life Center till her death of tuberculosis in 1906.

*

Louis and Fanny Pedersen came ashore in Seward on July 31, 1905 with a tent and four children, ages 3 to 12. They had about three months to get ready to spend the winter in that tent. This was insane.

If they felt betrayed or angry about the circumstances, they kept their lips sealed. This was the ultimate test of faith and idealism, their chance to make something of nothing. They were transferred here abruptly from a relatively easy two years in Douglas, across from Juneau on the other side of the gulf, where Louis had proven his mettle as a preacher by rebuilding a declining congregation.

Before leaving Douglas, Louis purchased an A-frame tent, 20 by 30 feet, which would be their home for the next two winters. He would improve the tent in stages and add other structures to ease their living situation.

Tents apparently were part of the frugal Methodist culture. In *Have Gospel Tent, Will Travel*, authors Bea Shepard and Claudia Kelsey quote another missionary, Carl Larsen, writing about his arrival in Dyea, starting point of the Chilkoot Trail, in 1897.

I am now busy setting up the tent Bishop McCabe gave me. Because of the strong winds constantly blowing here I am forced to lay a frame foundation to keep the tent from being torn away. I have bought a large stove, which I hope will give sufficient heat. My plans are to be ready for meetings in a week's time.

Seward when Louis and Fanny arrived was less than two years old, carved from the wilderness at the head of Resurrection Bay as a suitable, deep-water terminus for a railroad corridor that would move coal from the interior to the sea. Louis would soon become the railroad's official photographer, a sideline that brought the added benefit of ready access to the hard-living men who worked on it, as well as the East Coast industrial tycoons who came to inspect it.

But all this was yet to unfold. On that July day of 1905, Louis, Fanny, Fred, Ralph, Joe and Ruth walked uptown amid a landscape of rutted dirt streets littered with horse manure, bear scat and other debris to find a hotel for the night, till Louis could locate the church's land to pitch their tent. An article in the *Seward Phoenix Log* in July 1980 pinpoints the location as "the present 4th Avenue site of Michelle's and the bank parking lot." Seward's better streets in 1905 had planked sidewalks; sometimes two planks running parallel, with a big crack in between.

It was a settlement of rough shacks and cabins, the land logged in a hurry, with the stumps left to rot between houses in patches of Devil's Club. "There were stumps everywhere," Ruth Pedersen said. "They were the most wonderful places to play."

Drinking and prostitution were the main industries. Civic leaders and their wives had appealed to the Methodist Church to send a protestant preacher to assert some moral authority and civilizing influence on the town. John Parsons, superintendent of the church's Alaska mission writes in 1905:

Last August I went to the Westward as far as Seward. I secured the use of a vacant saloon building and preached to the people. Pious women in Seward had banded themselves together to pray for a minister to be sent to them and they regarded my coming as an answer to their prayer. There was no minister nearer

LOUIS AND FANNY

than Valdez, 150 miles away, and I promised them one in a few weeks.

Elsewhere Parsons adds:

The work of God has many difficulties peculiar to new communities, among which are the unsettled and changing population, the eager quest for wealth, the saloon with all its attendant evils of gambling and prostitution, and the dependence of the public schools for support upon the revenues derived from the sale of intoxicating drinks.

Louis and Fanny would quickly become pillars of Seward's aristocracy, as their daughter Ruts puts it. They were advocates of libraries and schools, and built important relationships with people of influence and means – industrialists, explorers, bankers, ship's captains and surveyors. They bridged all strata of the community from the privileged to the poor, ministering to prostitutes, prisoners, drunkards, loggers, hunters, and gold prospectors in the mountains who toiled alone in wilderness camps.

The Pedersen family stepped off the *SS Portland* at the foot of 4th Avenue, the town's main street, about a block from The Line, an alley between 2nd and 3rd Avenues that would soon be the focus of their battle against vice. It was the red-light district, and nothing Louis ever did quite shut it down. Not till World War II did the red lights go out, when the US military finally put an end to it.

Fanny dreaded Alaska. She and Louis asked the Methodist Church to send them to sweltering Africa or India, but the church had a special place in hell for them in the frozen north, living in a tent through the Alaska winter. Daughter Ruth said, "I recall my mother saying more than once that … all she could see was four little mounts of snow with four little while crosses above them. Later she would brag they had brought out six children with them, all alive and well."

The last frontier has always attracted people who fit nowhere else. Alaska is known as the place where a single woman could find a husband pretty easily. "The odds are good," the saying goes, "but the goods are odd." Many who gravitate to Alaska have a past, "and you don't ask about it."

A century ago, the hardships and difficulty facing the church in

Alaska were considered so great that the Methodist-Episcopal Church had determined it would treat the territory as though it were a foreign mission and not domestic. So Louis and Fanny were, in fact, missionaries. In 1904 the Methodists had only five such missionaries in coastal Alaska, stretched across a 2,000-mile picket line from Juneau to Unalaska, in the Aleutian Islands.

The Methodists had just five outposts in 2,000 miles of uninhabited wilderness. Louis and Fanny wouldn't get much help.

Chapter 3

An Inseparable Team

"My mother and father were inseparable," Ruth said. "She was always at Dad's side, supporting him with decisions, some of which were reached after heated discussion. She was an independent thinker, but had a quick smile and a gracious way of looking out for her kids and her family."

Ruth added, "She expected obedience from her children, but at the same time reassured us and made the whole adventure of Alaska a game, so that we didn't feel underprivileged in any way."

The game really shifted into high gear in Seward when they all lived in a tent through the winters of 1905 and 1906. Louis and Fanny had the character and backbone to do it.

Frances (Fanny) Turner Pedersen was a reformer and social activist – a warrior *against* alcohol and *for* women's equal rights in the suffrage movement. She was hauntingly beautiful, with brown eyes, brownish-blond hair and a kind, intelligent face.

Louis championed her causes every step of the way. She was at least his intellectual equal, possibly more, and he knew it. Fanny would become treasurer of the Alaska Women's Temperance Union. She knew all the state and national leaders and was friends with Frances Willard, the New York temperance reformer and suffragist; a guest in her home in Seward after Louis and Fanny finally built a house. In honor of her guest, Fanny named my uncle, her fifth child, Willard.

Louis was tall, upright and plainspoken. "I am a plain fellow with no handles on my name," he announced on cards he posted around Seward upon their arrival. As a frontier preacher he was not "bishop" or "doctor" anybody. His formal education was modest but his curiosity and ambition were large. He took pride in his talent at some worldly sidelines, especially photography, that helped put food on the table and children through college.

"He thinks he's a businessman," Fanny privately told Ruth, with a gleam in her brown eyes. "He needs a little straightening out once in a while."

Louis Klaus Olaus Haapstock Pedersen – Parson Pete – was both a preacher and a businessman, though preaching came first. From the pulpit he pointed the finger at sin wherever he saw it, even if it made the congregation squirm. "He'd pound the pulpit," Ruth said. "I'd sit there watching him and wonder, 'Who is he going to miss?'"

But she also saw another side – warmth and tenderness, a quick smile and a firm handshake – a father who loved to read and to sing. He taught his sons to remove their caps in the presence of women and get up from the table to pull out a chair for their mother. He believed in gracious little favors, bringing his wife a flower or an unexpected gift on return from a trip. "He never forgot," Ruth said.

And he loved to discuss the news.

"Our evening meal was always one of leisure time," Ruth said. "After we finished eating there was always conversation to finish and we took the time to listen to our father direct it into current events. He would quote from articles in the old *Literary Digest* and we'd get into discussions. Even the youngest in the family would participate."

He and Fanny loved the outdoors and led many day hikes together for visiting tourists. Sometimes they hiked by themselves to get away and talk.

The parson was at his best among the rough personalities of the railroad crews and backcountry camps, his son Joe said. Louis was a storyteller who could match any campfire tale, good or bad, with one of his own.

"He knew how to meet those men, how to talk to them," Joe said. "The parson met the men wherever he found them, ready to help and not find fault. He'd spell off a tree-faller with a double-bitted axe or pull one end of the six-foot framing saw. He would just visit a minute or two and pass on."

Louis was born into poverty in 1867. His father Klaus, a laborer, died of injuries after falling from a church steeple he was repairing, before his son was born. Louis came into the world on the steamer *North Star* off the coast of Norway while his mother, Anna, was en route to his father's bedside in Hammerfest.

Joe Pedersen explains:

News of the birth down in steerage became known throughout the little ship, and the circumstances of the mother's near-destitute situation. Wishing to help as best they could, the passengers and crew took up a collection and presented the new mother with a gift of silver coins. In her joy at the birth of a son and gratitude to the captain, passengers and crew, she included the captain's name in the name of her son and called him Klaus Olaus Haapstock Pedersen. Sometime later she engaged a silversmith to hammer out one of the coins to form a beautiful silver spoon, which she kept always in memory of the kind passengers and crew.

Louis's mother, Anna Groven Pedersen

Mother and son then emigrated to America in about 1869. Anna's sister emigrated ahead of her. Anna and Louis were living in Chicago during the great fire of 1871. When Louis was four, he and his mother moved west to Astoria, Oregon, where Louis grew up, received his education and became a U.S. citizen in return for his service in the Oregon State Militia.

"The militia," Joe Pedersen said, "was a bit like the Coast Guard – more or less a home guard. Any town of any size, and any state, had their militia in those days. They don't now, but at that time they had uniforms and guns and everything."

Anna Groven Pedersen crocheted fish nets for a living and, they say, enjoyed a cigar. She was so skilled at her craft that she was invited to demonstrate it at the San Francisco World's Fair, and did, at the Panama Pacific Internal Exposition of 1915.

Anna seems to have been married several times over the years, though the details are sketchy. At some point she married a fisherman, Johann M. Olsen, and referred to herself for the rest of

LOUIS AND FANNY

her life as Mrs. Captain J.M. Olsen. To the family she was Grandma Olsen.

Louis and Fanny

Louis was a student at the old Portland Military Academy and, as young man, worked in a grocery store and in the Astoria YMCA. After his service in the militia he enrolled in Portland Business College and that's where he met his eventual bride, the sheriff's daughter, the very beautiful Fanny. Her family was then living at Oysterville, at the far end of the Long Beach Peninsula. "I don't know how often he did it, but Dad told me he walked the 30-mile length of Long Beach to court mother," Joe Pedersen said. They were married in the Methodist-Episcopal Church in Oysterville, May 15, 1890.

By 1895 Louis had been ordained a minister of the Methodist Episcopal Church of the Oregon Conference, serving his first pastorates in Brooks and Silverton, just outside Salem. He was ordained a deacon in 1900 and an elder in 1902. That was the year the church sent him north to his first Alaska assignment in Douglas, across the channel from the state capitol of Juneau.

This was a transition time. The age of sail was winding down and the new age of industrialization and steam power was winding up. There were no automobiles, airplanes, radios, TVs, electric appliances, movie theatres nor electric power at all. Nor were there antibiotics. Railroads and steamships were the engines of progress. Horses and walking were everyday realities. Two great World Wars and a moon landing lay ahead in the new century.

Louis would gain much of his education by his own discipline, through a lifetime of reading and discussing books. He had a decent singing voice and a great love of music and favorite hymns of the day. Music was a way of life in the Pedersen home and singing was one of the strengths of his churches.

"One thing I remember particularly was those old, rough people coming into the church and sitting down, and oh how they sang," Joe Pedersen recalls. "I've never heard singing that impressed me as that singing did. Those fellows, some of them pretty rough characters, seemed to enjoy it, seemed to get a lot out of it."

Fanny brought quite a family heritage of her own to the partnership. She was the daughter of deeply religious Midwestern parents who moved West after the Civil War. Her father placed a high value on education and instilled this priority in all his children. Fanny attended business college in Portland, Oregon, where she met Louis.

A serious woman with a deep sense of duty, she is remembered also for a disarming sense of humor and plenty of confidence – sometimes misplaced – in her ability to think on her feet. For a time she worked as a hired girl for a family in Astoria, and one day the head of the household brought home a watermelon, the first Fanny had ever seen, to serve with the meal. Not wanting to admit she did not know how to prepare it, Fanny boiled the melon in water.

"They had a lot of fun with her on that one," Ruth replied.

To understand Fanny, it helps to understand her parents. Her mother, Martha Brownfield Turner, was a farm girl who married Fanny's father at age 15 while he was home on furlough from the

LOUIS AND FANNY

Fanny's Parents, Joseph and Martha Turner

Union Army during the Civil War. Fanny's father, Joseph, broke free of the dominant farm economy of the 1800s as a result of his military experience. He became sheriff and later postmaster in Pacific County, Washington. But his outlook on life really was shaped by the Civil War and his experience as a prisoner of war.

At 18 he traveled from the family home in Neoga, Illinois, to Springfield to enlist with the Union Army. He was assigned to Company H of the 48th Illinois Volunteers, serving with Grant and Sherman at Fort Henry, Fort Donaldson, Shiloh and the siege of Vicksburg before starting on Sherman's March to the Sea.

During the Battle of Atlanta, Turner was captured by Confederate forces and sent to the stockade at Andersonville, near Sumter, Georgia, where about a third of all Union prisoners died of malnutrition and disease.

At Andersonville he experienced two incredible strokes of luck. He was there when the Providence Spring erupted inside the camp, providing a new source of fresh water for the captives. And his capture came late in the war, when the Union finally agreed to some prisoner exchanges after resisting them for years. On September 17, 1864, Joseph was freed in a prisoner exchange and rejoined his unit and Sherman's March, to fight some more.

At the conclusion of Sherman's campaign, Turner's unit went north for the capture of Raleigh, the surrender of Johnston's army, and then of Lee, and finally the Grand Review at Washington.

He witnessed horrific slaughter and suffering on the battlefields. Thousands of wounded bled to death or died of infection who could have been saved by today's most rudimentary medical attention. Filth, disease, hunger and inhumanity at Andersonville Prison took additional thousands. To endure all this without losing his sanity or numbing himself with alcohol for the rest of his days called for immense strength.

Joseph's father was a blacksmith and a farmer on other people's land. His grandfather was a Methodist preacher named John Turner from New Jersey who fought in the American Revolution, according to sketchy notes in the Turner family Bible. So the heritage of Methodism, patriotism and service ran deep in the Turner family, extending not only to Joseph Turner but also to his children including Fanny.

Her family had played a role in shaping the entire history of the young nation beginning with the Revolutionary War, and the job wasn't quite finished yet, and Fanny aimed to put her touches on it in the areas of prohibition and suffrage.

John Wesley Turner, Fanny's Uncle

Of all those who influenced Fanny's father, Joseph, the foremost seems to have been his older brother, John Wesley Turner, known usually as Wesley. He was the religious leader of the extended family, an "exhorter" in the Methodist-Episcopal Church and also a part-time country doctor and snake oil salesman. Medicine was a craft he learned apparently by apprenticing, since there were no medical schools. Joseph wrote Wesley many times during the Civil War and some of those letters have survived in family attics. They reflect great brotherly affection and warmth.

Wesley and his young wife, Harriett Smith Turner, came west on the Oregon trail in the last year of the Civil War, 1865 and homestead on 160 acres of grasslands near Goldendale, in south central Washington. And then he wrote letters begging Joseph and his young wife, Fanny, to follow.

"If you would take my advice, you would leave that old lease in 24 hours and come out to the rich pastures of Washington where you can have a farm of your own and live like a gentleman, and be somebody, too," he wrote Joseph.

Apparently Joseph found the advice persuasive, because in 1871 he and Fanny's mother, and one-year-old Fanny, left Illinois on the new transcontinental railroad for San Francisco, then made their way north to homestead near La Center, Washington. Within a few years they moved to the Long Beach peninsula where Fanny grew up and her dad worked a series of occupations including oyster farmer and hotelkeeper, moving up to territorial sheriff and later postmaster at South Bend.

An incident in Turner's jail, April 11, 1891, profoundly shamed Fanny's father. Raiders came ashore in the county seat of Oysterville during the night, overpowered the jail guard and executed two accused murderers.

"I am humiliated and half insane," he wrote in a note summoning help. A man of deep honor, Turner never ran again for reelection, becoming postmaster instead, in South Bend, a job he held till his death at the young age of 62 in 1905, of a heart attack. The community gave him a hero's funeral, one of the largest ever held.

Fanny's World

Willard R. Espy paints a colorful picture of the world in which Fanny grew to young womanhood in his 1977 masterpiece, *Oysterville*.

The village was divided between the saved and the damned, with the damned, I am afraid, frequently in the majority. ... The county seat in the seventies and eighties was a magnet for the lawless element up and down the coast, particularly the drinkers, the gamblers, and the type of young lady who favored their company. Oysters fed them all. When the oyster business collapsed and the county seat was kidnapped a few years later, not only the business establishments but the saloons and dance halls vanished overnight from Oysterville. ...By the time my own parent made their permanent home there in 1902, the village, or what was left of it, was as stuffed with piety as a dying atheist.

Espy zeros in especially on the Methodist Church in Oysterville, where the Turners were stalwart members. *"… The decent element of Oysterville was in at least nominal charge. Its visible symbol, from 1872 on, was the Methodist Church.*

He continues, *"The part of the Oysterville population that was damned spent much of its time directly across the street from the church, in the saloon that occupied a wing of the Pacific Hotel. …During court week it served as many as 250 customers a day. When the Methodist church was formally opened, Richard Caruthers, owner of the Pacific Hotel, closed its doors for the duration of the ceremonies so that his parishioners could pay their respects to the Lord. When the blessings were over, the Methodists and the tosspots alike repaired to the saloon.*

At Rodway's Saloon *"…It is said that no woman ever pushed open its swinging door except to wield a hatchet on the bottles, or to drag home an errand husband."*

Fanny would get her turn to wield a hatchet on the saloons of Alaska.

The tent church in 1905. *Louis Pedersen photo*

Chapter 4

The Tent

"I thought it was quite a lark, you know, for a youngster who didn't know anything else," Ruth Pedersen said of living in a tent for two winters.

Earliest photographs show a mostly canvas structure on a mound of dirt and cobble, nestled amid scrub trees and logs. Low sidewalls reinforced the base, but its most distinctive feature was a prominent, hand-lettered sign over the door: Methodist Episcopal Church, ALL WELCOME.

Their transfer here was rather sudden, after an easy two years in Douglas, across the Gastineau Channel from Juneau. In Douglas in 1903, Louis took over an established church with a declining attendance and turned it around.

Mission Superintendent John Parsons explained in his 1904 and 1905 reports, "The work here is very difficult because a large part of the population are foreigners who neither speak our language or (sic) understand our ways, and because of the general disregard of the Lord's Day."

He went on, "At the end of last year it was thought we should give up Douglas, but nobody is so minded now. Bishop Hamilton sent L.H. Pedersen to Douglas last year and he needs no words of commendation from me. His works praise him."

Joe Pedersen said Douglas was where he first realized his dad's influence. "Dad and I were walking on the sidewalk between Douglas and the mine, and as we walked along we met some of these Slavs, people of foreign origin. When they saw the minister coming, they got off the sidewalk and took off their hats and bowed their heads as we went by."

"I thought, boy, my Dad must be somebody! Ralph tells me when Dad landed in Douglas he had a bolero hat. I know he also had a twisted-up moustache, and I guess he made quite an impression."

Presumably, this was why Louis's bosses chose him for the new challenge of Seward.

"As soon as he had his church up (in Seward)," Joe Pedersen said, "people came. He had a way with rough mining people and prospectors. He seemed to know how to meet them, how to talk to them."

Ruth agreed. "I think my father liked a challenge. His best work was where he met people stripped of their superficialities – bedrock, down to the quick of life. He had a ready smile and a quick realization of the needs of other people."

Louis posted signs around town. *Hello! Just heard you're to be in Seward a few days. What do you say to going to the Methodist Church next Sunday? The preacher – a plain fellow without handles to his name – and everybody there will be glad to see you. Good singing, too. L.H. Pedersen, Pastor.*

For about three weeks the family lived in one end of the church tent – a 10-foot section portioned off at the back. Joe Pedersen explains, "We had some kind of drapery we would pull, and the church was held in the front end of it. We did not have a house to live in so Dad had to build a little shed which was to be our dormitory."

In the dormitory Louis built bunk beds. Fred, Ralph and Joe slept on the upper bunks – Louis, Fanny and Ruth slept below.

For the first two winters, Ruth says, "First thing Dad would do every morning was pick up the corners of the tarp that covered the lower bunk and shake the snow out onto the floor. Then he would take a broom and sweep the snow outside that had accumulated during the night, and then start the fire."

Cooking and dining in such a limited space was nearly impossible so, Joe Pedersen says, "Dad put up another tent next to the dormitory that was our kitchen and dining room. We often wore full outdoor wraps including mittens when we ate our meals."

Eventually, Louis boarded up all the buildings, "But not too tightly," Joe adds, "because snow and cold sure came in when the wind blew. Ruth and I had many a happy time sliding down the dormitory shed roof in Mother's wooden chopping bowl. When the bowl parted ways the sliding ended and Mother got a nice, new chopping bowl."

A small heater and kitchen stove with an oven enabled the family to heat rocks, which they wrapped in old blankets and took to bed at

The tent parsonage in March 1906. *Louis Pedersen photo*

The church fully enclosed in late 1905, with family living quarters now in the tent next door.

night in the dormitory to provide extra warmth under the covers."

Townspeople soon turned out to fully enclose the original church tent with lumber. The *Seward Daily Gateway* reported that by November 5, 1905, the church had become a shiplap structure built over the tent frame. The parsonage was the tent next door. According to the *Gateway*, volunteers assisted Louis and his oldest son, Fred, in finishing the wood-frame church. This work had begun as a modest effort to make the tent warmer and give it a roof that could bear the weight of snow.

A Dr. Sleem in Seward had suggested the Methodist Society make a complete frame structure and he set about raising the funds personally. *The Gateway* reported, "The new structure is boarded on all sides and has a layer of heavy paper to give it added warmth. The roof is shingled and the building is to have a rustic front with a layer of shiplap. The big canvas tent will be sold to help raise money to pay for the lumber which has gone into the building."

Volunteers contributing carpentry were John Zeigler, A.J. Sheff, T.R. Wilson, D.C. Brownell Jr., and Fred Brown.

Louis was constantly improving the church building, Ruth says. "With his own hands he made benches for people to sit on. The benches had no backs – you just sat on rough, wooden benches. In time he got backs on them, too."

Ruth says the church attracted so many attendees because her father was able to meet the people of the community one-to-one, and passed no judgment. "Of course in Alaska nobody has a past. I'm not suggesting we carried one, but you never asked questions of anybody."

An article in the *Seward Phoenix Log* remarked on how productive Louis was during this time. "Living in cramped quarters and doing lots of construction seems to have scant effect on Reverend Pederson's (sic) preaching. Besides Sunday Services at the church, he managed to preach every other Sunday at the jail, too."

And he was setting up schools. The Nov. 11, 1907 Seward Daily Gateway reported, "All persons interested in the taking up of the 9th grade school work, which is the first year's work in high school, during the coming year are requested to see Rev. L.H. Pedersen." His own son, Fred, would become Seward's first high school graduate.

Methodist parsonage foreground, with Mt. Marathon behind. *Louis Pedersen photo*

DAN PEDERSEN

1908 – Moving Into the Parsonage

Early in 1908 the family left the tent behind and moved into an honest-to-goodness parsonage Louis built on Church Street. Bea Shepard and Claudia Kelsey, in their book, *Have Gospel Tent Will Travel*, report the lumber came from an Alaska Railway bunkhouse Pedersen purchased.

"The foundation and basement were constructed of logs," Joe Pedersen said. "This later proved just the right thing to withstand the frequent earthquakes that occur in Seward. The superstructure was a 1-1/2 story, double-constructed frame. Ruth had her bedroom. We three boys shared a bedroom, and Mother and Dad had a bedroom. We lived in luxury! We even had a real water closet in the basement, with a high water tank with a long pull chain."

The move coincided perfectly with Kodak's introduction of real photo postcard paper and enabled Louis to embark seriously on his photography hobby turned business.

He now had a residence with space for darkroom equipment in the basement. He could also now create a new form of entertainment for Seward, slide shows using images he exposed on plates of glass and then color-tinted and projected onto a screen with a glass lantern projector.

Louis was appointed official photographer of the Alaska Central Railway and documented construction of much of the first 70 miles of track from Seward, two-thirds of the way to Anchorage. Many of his images are circulated widely today on the Internet without attribution. He also sold post cards to tourists. By the time the family moved to Skagway in 1913, photography had become a significant business not only for Louis but several of the older Pedersen boys. Fred and Ralph would operate a photography studio in Skagway.

No wonder Fanny had to remind him, from time to time, what his real business was.

Resurrection Bay. *Louis Pedersen photo*

Chapter 5

The Parson's Picture Show

The crowd that turned out in Seward one winter evening of 1908 was looking forward to something special. Tonight they would forget the chill and isolation of this remote Alaska settlement and embark on a journey of the imagination.

A hush fell over the audience as ushers on both sides of the church caught the signal to dim the gas lamps. All eyes turned to the lanky figure at the center of the room, busy now in the shadows over a boxy metal contraption with a long snout and a chimney. It smelled of hot metal, and a wisp of oil smoke curled up from its center column.

Stacked nearby were three black boxes about a foot long, holding 82 small plates of glass, each in its own velvet-lined compartment.

Louis straightened up and looked around at the suddenly quiet crowd anticipating hi words. He held a three-by-four inch glass plate in his hand, ready for the moment of drama.

He cleared his throat.

"Most people love to travel," he began. "Often, when the boat is about to pull off from the wharf with friends on board, we have wished we might join them in seeing the sights of the world."

These are his exact words. He practiced his timing, wrote them all down, and even created a long version and a short version of his "Around the World" show.

On this winter night, long before the era of television, movie theatres and motion pictures, Pedersen made some magic. He took his audience on a flight of fancy all the way around the world, to strange and exotic places even he had never been. In 60 minutes, or 75 if he included all his jokes, he cast a spell in this darkened room that left his friends and neighbors talking for weeks about the strange and wonderful entertainment they'd seen.

The technology that made this possible was the magic lantern, predecessor of today's slide and movie projectors. The ungainly device employed a high intensity oil lamp positioned between a lens and a mirror.

With its high heat and open flame it was a bit dangerous, which may have added to its mystique. Fingers could get burned. But it could throw photographic images from hand-tinted plates of glass through the lens onto a screen, a process that delighted and thrilled most viewers who could barely conceive how the enlarged images got there.

Magic lanterns were manufactured in many shapes and configurations, some of which bore a striking resemblance to a mechanical camel or Trojan horse.

Pedersen likened the lantern to an enchanted horse he had read about in the book, *Arabian Nights Entertainments*. In the story, Pedersen recalled, a Hindu visits the Sultan of Persia. "Accompanying the Hindu was a remarkable horse made of wood, but so lifelike it was taken for real by many," Pedersen told the audience. "On mounting this horse the Hindu need but wish to go anywhere, and by turning a little peg concealed in the neck of the horse it would rise into the air and go in the direction desired, and by turning another peg it would descend to the ground," much as he would tonight insert and remove the 3x4-inch plates of glass from the box in front of him.

"Let us imagine ourselves accompanying our young friends," he began. "And accepting the camera, the lantern and the printed page as our enchanted horse, we shall cross continents and seas, visit many strange places and peoples; and without serious danger from submarines below, the belching battleship nearby or the dropping of bombs from above, we shall return without having fed the fishes or become poor through tipping the waiters."

My god, where the heck was he going with this?

"We wish to be upon a passenger steamer leaving New York; and …

"Presto!" he exclaimed, inserting the first slide. "Here we are!"

(Author's note: Finally!)

Thus began his narrated show of 82 image taking the audience from New York City to Europe and Russia, to the Holy Land, the pyramids of Egypt, to India, China and Japan, and home across the Pacific to the rich and diverse wonders of North America, ending in a flurry of patriotism and love of country.

Louis called the show "Around the World in Sixty Minutes," and after premiering it in Seward in 1908, he repeated it for the Seward audience again in 1912 and took it on the road – the sea, actually – to Nome later that year, where it surely must have been quite a community event for townspeople and natives living in such isolation in a truly remote corner of the frontier.

He presented "Around the World" at least seven times. On the envelope in which he kept the script he scribbled the date of each showing. The list includes one show in Skagway in 1915 and three more after he left Alaska, in the Washington communities of Snohomish and Everett late in 1925, and Monroe early in 1926.

Jokes are a part of any good speaker's repertoire and Louis peppered his narrative with the humor of his day, which he gleaned from voracious reading of magazines. Much of what typified this era's magazines, newspapers and daily discourse would be inappropriate, insensitive and offensive by today's standards. As he projected a slide of China on the screen, Pedersen remarked, "Some speak of these people as the Yellow Peril. 'Look here,' exclaimed an American wife and she read the daily. 'I see from statistics given here that every third baby born in the world is a Chinese. Is that so, Mary? Well, let's thank the Lord this is only our first.'"

More revealing, though, was the lavish praise this self-made, naturalized American heaped on his adopted land – for the diverse beauty of its many states, its inspiring Capitol and republican system of government, its President and Congress.

He ended his photographic world tour with these thoughts:

"In fancy we have visited many lands, but to us there is none so inviting as our own. Our closing thought is expressed in the words of Henry Van Dyke: 'Oh, it's home again, and home again. America for me! I want a ship that's Westward bound to plow the rolling sea. To the blessed land of Room Enough beyond the ocean bars, where the air is full of sunshine and the flag is full of stars.'"

Louis used the magic lantern as a tool throughout his career to attract audiences and add impact to important stories. His grandson, Joe Finrow Pedersen, owns a collection of glass slides containing the verses of hymns Louis projected during church services and meetings. Just a year after Louis first presented "Around the World" in Seward, he traveled all the way to New York City with his projector to present a very special slide show about Alaska. It was a one-man public relations and fund-raising campaign that was a spectacular success. More on that later.

Louis's job as photographer for the railroad gave him access not only the laborers but also to Eastern industrialists who could help fund his work in Seward. He photographed this party at Kern Creek in August 1911.

Chapter 6

Following the Rails

By 1908, events were in motion that would take Louis to the streets of New York City in a fur parka and mukluks, holding a sign.

He was not only mastering the projector and holding services but also running the Seward library in one end of the church and getting to know the railroad crews. He picked up a side job as the railroad's photographer.

Joe Pedersen tells the story in some undated, handwritten notes he prepared for a talk about his dad.

"In Seward, the little tent church was well established. It had grown in service, as well as now being a fully boarded-up, shingle-roofed structure with a lean-to addition that served as the town library six days a week, and as space for Sunday School on Sunday.

"When the railroad men came to town," Joe says, "some of them divided their time between the 13 saloons down the street and the church 'up the street.' Some, of course, found it impossible to make it up the hill, but the Parson met the men wherever he found them, always ready to help and never to judge."

Building the railroad was a steeper challenge than the Ballaine brothers ever anticipated. A perfect storm of problems confronted them – "the decline of the Gold Rush, the total absence of a population along the route, the 2,000-mile boat haul for every pound of food, equipment and supplies, plus the fact that Seward had little to offer by way of support besides the doubtful worth of its 13 saloons."

Furthermore, "The severity of winter snows, cold and wind seemed to oppose every move of man and beast for half of every year. With all these factors and more to buck against it, it is little wonder that six years later there were only 49 miles of track in service."

But in 1908 things looked up a bit, Joe says. "New financing was secured, the workforce was increased, and the camp at Mile 49 was humming. The Parson felt again that urge to get out among the men. It was here at Mile 49 that the railroad established a larger, somewhat permanent camp capable of caring for about 150 men. There were bunkhouses, cook shack, storage shed, blacksmith shop and a machine shop. It was here also that the engineers were faced with a very difficult piece of construction, a timber trestle more than half a mile in length, shaped much like a handwritten 'e' or loop, which turned back under itself."

This was fertile ground for Louis. "So, with his fold-up, suitcase-like reed organ and an armload of songbooks, Dad boarded the 'Toonerville Trolley' for the camp at Mile 49. During the day he visited among the men wherever he found them – in the woods, building the right-of-way, building the trestle. Often he would spell off a tree-faller with the double-bitted axe or pull one end of the six-foot framing saw."

Louis entered into story telling with enthusiasm. "He became well known as a story teller who always had a 'true' story to match every one someone else had to tell," Joe said.

Ruth adds that in addition to visiting the railroad men, her dad also hiked into the mountains in the summertime to visit miners at their remote claims. "Dad would go off on a trek every summer – taking with him usually one of the boys. Father and son would get to know each other in a way they wouldn't otherwise. Dad learned a great deal of woods lore. He'd usually be gone about two weeks with a backpack, hunting up these lonely men who were out in the hills all by themselves. For them, the sight of a fellow human being was a ray of sunshine."

Not only did these hikes deepen the bond between father and son, they built a relationship with the miners. "Dad got very close to these lonely men," Ruth said. "They had a great understanding of each other. I always felt my father's greatest work as a minister was when he carried the gospel to these people," Ruth said. "His attributes were along the lines of pioneering rather than the formal, organized church. He liked the pioneer atmosphere, the openness. He felt he was one of them."

In return, the men sought Louis out. "During the long winter months the miners would often walk back to town and we got to know many characters – One Eyed Charlie, Old Man Bill, Johnny the Janitor."

Ruth continued, "They relished coming to the parsonage, maybe having a home-cooked meal, being part of the family life for an evening and feeling they weren't altogether outcasts. Many of these men had come up to Alaska as a last resort, either to end it all or forget the past."

A curious article about the Pedersens' experience in Alaska appeared in a 1908 issue of the Sunday school newspaper, *Classmate*, published by Eaton & Mains of New York. The newspaper describes itself as an illustrated paper of eight pages, published weekly for young people.

Quoting from the article, Children of Alaska: "It seems a little strange that a minister and his family could live in a tent all winter and be comfortable in a latitude of sixty degrees." (Fanny might dispute the comfort.) And yet our pastor, the Rev. L.H. Pedersen, and family, enjoyed life where persons at the southeastern end of Greenland would call it stinging cold.

"Up in Alaska there are always some features new and strange to be reckoned with, not down on the program of the usual services in the home churches. One cold night the tabernacle church was crowded and the revival was going on splendidly when a belated hearer found nor seat or room and so he strayed into the adjoining parsonage and sat down on the edge of a bed where he could hear, if not see, all that was going on.

"The warm room, the inviting couch, persuaded him to tip over and go to sleep. When the good pastor and family returned from church, there on the bed was a great, strong man fast asleep who, when awakened, felt no embarrassment for having had a comfortable nap."

The article reflected, no doubt, Louis's quest for publicity – to put his Seward mission on the map and attract nationwide attention and funding.

The Dec. 6, 1908, issue of *Classmate* included a photo Louis took of Fanny, as musher of a small dog team, with Ruth and Joe standing beside the lead dog.

1909-1910: The Triumphant Trip Outside

But the real publicity push came in the summer of 1909 when Louis earned a one-year sabbatical in return for five years of service. He and Fanny planned to use it for a mixture of business and pleasure on a long family vacation from the rigors of the north.

Several of their children would attend the Alaska Yukon Pacific Exposition under way on the grounds of the University of Washington in Seattle. All four of the children exhibited samples of their schoolwork at the expo – Fred and Ralph at the high school level, and Joe and Ruth in the primary school exhibit. The family then proceeded to Salem, Oregon, where the children resided with family friends during the 1909-1910 school year while Louis and Fanny traveled on to the Midwest and New York City.

In Chicago, New York City and elsewhere, Louis put on a one-man PR blitz to raise financing for a YMCA for Seward. A big part of his ministry had been to the single men and loners who had no wholesome place to live and relax in Seward – only the saloons and houses of prostitution. He saw a YMCA as part of the answer to this need.

The Seward Community Library tracked Pedersen's travels in an index of articles published in the *Seward Daily Gateway:*

- 29 January 1910: Doing publicity work in states
- 5 March 1910: Lectures in Chicago
- 19 March 1910: In New York City
- 26 March 1910: Booms Seward in Astoria
- 28 May 1910: Alameda passenger (returning to Seward with Fanny, Fred, Ralph, Joe and Ruth)

Guests of a New York City Financier

The New York City stop was momentus. Every summer, parties of tourists traveled up the coast of Alaska, many getting to know Louis and Fanny in Seward, coming to their home to order post cards. In 1909, the steamer *Yucatan* arrived with the traveling party of a New York City financier, George W. Perkins, a partner in J.P. Morgan's banking firm from 1901-1910. Among members of his party were his wife, Evelina Ball; his sister, a Mrs. Brewster; Dorothy Perkins and Mrs. Emily Perkins.

Perkins, in his 40s, was already a businessman of substance prior to his partnership with J.P. Morgan. He had been vice president of New York Life Insurance Company from 1892-1903, and during his career served on the boards of the International Mercantile Marine Company, U.S. Steel Corporation and International Harvester.

The website Bookrags.com sheds light on Perkins' influence. In the early 1900s, the telephone was just gaining acceptance in the business world. Bookrags states, "At the present time, the banker who works closest to the telephone is probably George W. Perkins of the J.P Morgan group of bankers. He is the only man," says Morgan, "who can raise twenty millions in twenty minutes."

Ruth recalls Perkins believed in supporting missionary work. He heard about Louis and Fanny's activities in Seward and wanted to see for himself when he visited the city to size up the Alaska Central Railway. The Perkins section of the *Seward Weekly Gateway* index for 1909-10 sketches the picture. Note especially the final entry:

- 10 July: On Alaska Tour
- 17 July: On business for Morgan
- 17 July: The Perkins tour
- 31 July: In Seward
- 31 July: Examines ACR (Alaska Central Railway) for purchase
- 07 Aug: Fishes and Spawns Rumors
- 28 Aug: Meets Bankers at Sea
- 28 Aug: Thinks Well of Alaska
- 02 Oct: Boosts Alaska's Resources
- 16 Oct: Rumors Gratifying if True
- 16 Oct: Talks of Alaska Coal
- 13 Nov: Wall St. Journal says Perkins and Morgan bought ACR
- 21 May: Ballinger-Perkins Letters Revealed
- 04 June: Contributes to Seward YMCA

Relations between the Pedersens and Perkins blossomed during their visit to Seward, according to Ruth. "They were in port for two or three days, and the Perkins party and my father and mother became fast friends. Mr. Perkins learned of my father's desire to establish a YMCA in Seward to benefit the single men, chiefly, who had no place to go – no recreation available except the saloons. Dad felt that if there were only a YMCA that was clean and mostly furnished, it would provide something desirable for these single men."

LOUIS AND FANNY

When it came time for Louis and Fanny to take their sabbatical leave, Perkins helped finance the trip. "It became quite an event in our family," Ruth said. "It was 1909 when the Alaska Yukon Pacific Exposition was being held in Seattle. My mother, brother Joe and I came out first and topped in Seattle to attend the fair – a great event in our lives. Then we were joined about three months later by my father and two older brothers. We were taken to Salem, Oregon, where Fred and Ralph were placed in Willamette Academy, living in a private home. My brother Joe and I were domiciled in another private home and placed in grade school while my folks went back to New York City and stayed in the home of the George W. Perkins family."

Paradise on the Hudson

This would have been in the breathtaking splendor of Glyndor House, part of the Perkins estate on a commanding site overlooking the Palisades of the Hudson River in the Bronx. George and Evelina purchased the villa, called Nonesuch, from Oliver Harriman in 1895. They remodeled and enlarged the house with guest rooms and a ballroom.

In 1903 they added onto their estate by purchasing the adjacent Wave Hill House, which today is a city-owned garden and center of the arts, culture, environment and horticulture. The constructed a tunnel from Glyndor House to a new, two-story recreation building they built at Wave Hill, complete with billiard room, bowling alley and squash court.

The Perkins estate must have stirred the emotions of Louis with his vision of a humble YMCA for Seward. The recreation building's roof was covered with sod to provide a terrace from which to enjoy the view of the Hudson and the Palisades. The Perkins family added greenhouses, gardens, and an outdoor swimming pool, and lovingly landscaped the grounds. This was the Garden of Eden in which Louis and Fanny spent the summer of 1909 – a setting today called "an oasis of serenity" in New York City.

The contrast between such affluence and the privation of Alaska must have been staggering to Louis and Fanny. The New York City attorney William Lewis Morris had built Wave Hill. It was used as a summer residence by William Henry Appleton, a world-renowned publisher, and leased in the early 1870 by Teddy Roosevelt Sr., whose young son, later President, gained a lifelong love of nature here. Just prior to its purchase by Perkins the home had been leased by Mark Twain for two years, who filled its halls with a procession of literary artists. Charles Darwin was a visitor. It was later home to conductor Arturo Toscanini.

From this exalted setting, Louis embarked on a one-man campaign in New York City to attract attention to Alaska and raise financing for his proposed YMCA. Ruth continues, "While in New York City my dad gave illustrated lectures on Alaska. He would dress in a fur parka and mukluks and walk down the streets of New York City carrying a banner which said, 'All About Alaska – See the Beautiful Pictures.' The banner told where and what time. He would often be followed by a string of dogs sniffing at his mukluks and looking a bit cowed at the smell that emanated, but his lectures were well attended and the money came in from somewhere. I think he took a collection."

The parson showed pictures he had taken himself and made into glass slides, which he colored and projected.

"Mr. Perkins himself was a heavy contributor to the YMCA project," Ruth says. "Enough money was raised that upon my parents' return they picked up their family in Salem, Oregon, and we all traveled back to Alaska on the Alameda, as I recall."

Louis purchased a large building near the beach, just across from where the boats landed, and built his YMCA. He hired a caretaker, "Brother Bill," who kept the building clean and maintained. "There was no rowdyism," Ruth said. "It was well patronized by the community."

The Perkins family remained engaged and kept in touch with the Pedersen family for many years. "They made substantial gifts," Ruth said, "usually at Christmas or some other time when they just felt the urge."

Perkins died in 1920 at the age of 58, just two years after the Pedersens left Alaska, but Mrs. Brewster, especially, continued to remember Joe and Ruth.

"About the time I graduated from eighth grade she sent me a ring with three small diamonds in it," Ruth said, "and about a year later she sent me a ring with a square-cut emerald. That was really something for a poor little missionary girl way up in Alaska. She stipulated I was to have them at the present time and enjoy wearing them, and that when the time came for my education I was to use them for that purpose if I needed the money."

Louis and Fanny's trip to New York City was so successful that, about this time, they started aiming higher than jut a YMCA for Seward. They were thinking in broader terms of a network of YMCA's throughout Alaska. The *Seward Weekly Gateway* of June 4, 1910, reports that, "through Mr. Pedersen's efforts, official representatives of the Young Men's Christian Association will visit parts of Alaska next year and, as a result, it is expected that an organization will be established in several places, including Seward.

"A noticeable need in every Alaskan town is a place for recreation and social resort," the *Gateway* reported. "Every church in the territory feels this, and has made more or less of an effort to supply it." As soon as a suitable building could be rented in Seward it would be filled with a good reading room, gymnastic apparatus, game rooms, billiards "and other attractions appealing to men," and possibly a small lunch counter where a cup of hot coffee and a sandwich could be purchased.

Less than two months later, on July 30, 1910, the *Gateway* reported Rev. L.H. Pedersen, "representing a branch of the YMCA to be established in Seward," had completed purchase from F.L. Ballaine of a building formerly occupied by the Seward Commercial Company.

"The structure is on the ground owned by the Alaska Northern, but the company will charge no ground rent and the building will be permitted to remain at its present location until such time as the lot is required for other purposes… A gymnasium and games of various kinds will be installed and a cozy reading room fixed up, having on it tables many of the leading newspapers, magazines and periodicals. The equipment has already been ordered and the YMCA will be opened to the public on Sept. 1."

This photo Louis took of a Black Bear and a Grizzly squaring off was published worldwide and appeared in *National Geographic* magazine in November 1916.

Chapter 7

Playing With Bears

Some things demand urgent attention:

- Cataclysmic volcanic eruption
- Your house on fire
- Bears playing with your little girl

Miners in the backcountry, to whom Fanny would send a fresh-baked loaf of bread in Louis's backpack, sometimes felt compelled to return

LOUIS AND FANNY

Ruth, in the jail yard, plays with her bears. The caption Louis etched on this image was "More – we're awful hungry!"

the favor. "These men would (work) the outlying mines for weeks at a time, trying to prove their claim," Ruth said. "They had to do something to help pass the time.

"They wanted to say thank you for the homemade bread my mother sent to them. It wouldn't be proper to give a gift to the minister's wife," she said, "so the youngster got it. I was the only daughter."

"One miner brought me, oh, the most enchanted little house I've ever laid eyes on – about three or four feet long and two feet wide – a perfect little log house made of the limbs of little willow trees. Another one gave me a watch – many gifts, music, even goodies the miners would bake themselves.

Of all the gifts, nothing came close to the twin bear cubs.

"Those bears were one of the gifts they brought me," Ruth said. "We had them several weeks, chained to large stones or blocks over in the jail yard. We would go over every day with food from our house and play with them. Later, I was criticized for it because the hunter said they were very dangerous.

"I have one picture of a bear on my back. I thought, 'Oh, this is a nice little affectionate bear,' but the hunter said it was dangerous because, with one slap of its paw, it could take out an eye. We finally sent them off to Woodland Park Zoo in Seattle."

But first, Louis got some classic photographs of Ruth with the bears that now reside in the Seward Community Library and online on Wikimedia Commons.

But this wasn't the family's only brush with bears. The railroad figured in another memorable incident.

"One summer our family and one or two others joined forces to go on a camping trip out to Mile 34 (about four miles beyond Moose Pass) on the Alaska Central Railroad," Ruth said. "There were a couple of men who were hunters. Billy Lowell, the half-breed Indian, was our guide and main hunter. A hand-pumped handcar was our means of locomotion."

It was a great morning when the group piled all its gear onto the

LOUIS AND FANNY

handcar. "We youngsters were allowed to sit on the edge with our feet hanging over while the men took turns pumping that car for 34 miles."

Before leaving town, the newspaper editor, Mr. Shaw, approached Fanny's parents and said he was worried about them going out to Mile 34 in the hill country and bear country with no more protection than these hunters. "He said he would feel better if we had a dog with us who knew how to handle bears, so he wanted to lend us his dog Prince to keep with us as long as we were on the camping trip.

"Now Prince was a beautiful, big dog and came along," Ruth said.

"He understood he was our dog for a few days. I don't recall whether he rode or hiked all that distance. I think he hiked a good way."

The group made it to Mile 34 and the men pitched the tents while the women made up the beds. "Everybody fixed a little fire in front of their tent to make the evening meal. I remember my mother making powder biscuits and cooking them over the bonfire in what they called a little reflector. They were awfully good.

"That night, porcupines visited us. Prince didn't think that was very funny so he scrounged into the tent with the rest of us.

"The next morning the hunters went out to see if they could find any sign of bear, and pretty soon one came back and said he'd found tracks. 'We're going to get a bear!' Everyone was excited. Prince stood up on his four legs and his tail went up in the air. He looked a little suspicious but went with the hunters and the men, trailing the bear. They followed the bear's tracks through the shrubs and bushes and finally came to a clearing, all muddy, and the first thing they knew, here was some mud up ahead that was still steaming!

"They knew they were right on the heels of that bear. Prince went forward and smelled that mud and his tail went down with a bang between his legs. His head went down almost touching his two front feet, and he headed back for camp.

"When the hunters got back with the bear, where was Prince? Nobody knew. Prince had absolutely disappeared. We couldn't find Prince anywhere – didn't know what to do. Couldn't find him. We were sure the bears had gotten him, but it turns out Prince had gone back to town (on his own) and never stopped till he got home again.

"Mr. Shaw apologized for his dog's bad manners."

Ruth commented that the Episcopal Church had gone into Seward just ahead of the Methodist and there was a very fine relationship between the two. The Catholic Church was there also, "and again, there was a very warm feeling among the three congregations.

"The Methodist Church was more or less the social center of the town. The Ladies Aid Society would have ice cream socials. They would have Japanese teas. It was really quite a social center and they managed to have enough events that they raised a little money and bought an organ for the church – a little foot-pumped organ. They also bought a bell for the church to mount on a high, delicate post. It was quite historic because it became the fire alarm for the town, too."

The Pedersens would get a chance to ring it one winter night sometime later when their own house burned down.

Much camaraderie exited among the churches, Ruth said. The public Christmas tree was put up in the Methodist Church. Gifts were brought to the church and placed on the tree, and that's where the gift exchange took place. Santa Claus arrived with a dog team and sleigh bells, and entered by the north window. "And always the Catholic Church had their Christmas exercise. The Methodist minister's children were invited and there was always a gift on the tree for each of the Methodist youngsters, which we thought was a very nice touch, especially if it had popcorn in it."

About once a month a boat would arrive from Seattle. "Seward was the terminus of the run, and on arrival in Seward the ship would usually stay one full night, possibly two, waiting for the townspeople to pick up their mail, read it, answer it and get it back on the same boat. Of course, freight came in and had to be unloaded for town supplies. Everything in town stopped for the arrival of the boat."

"In the summertime if there were tourists aboard, there would usually be a dance hastily put together, which was held above the old Brown & Hawkins Store. There was a dance hall and my parents always went."

Brown & Hawkins was a mercantile store that sold groceries, miners' supplies and haberdashery. Ruth said someone usually sat at the piano. "A few times my parents permitted me to go to this dance, knowing it was not the thing for good Methodists to do, but still realizing that it was an event of the town that was important socially and couldn't be all bad. So my folks would go down and stay through the first dance. Having made an appearance and being recognized, made to feel really a part of the social life of the town, they would depart."

DAN PEDERSEN

The Preacher's Darkroom

Louis had many interests besides missionary work, Ruth points out. "He was a very skilled photographer and supplemented his missionary income by making postcards in wholesale quantities.

"With the arrival of the boat in Seward during tourist season, tourists would come to the house and my folks would get out the large sample albums with postcards – scenes of the mountains in their grandeur, mountains and water, ships, maybe the ship on which they'd just arrived. Often, these tourists would include reporters for newspapers or magazines.

"They would come up to the parsonage – by this time we were in a nice home – and give their orders for so many hundred of these cards. This meant that my father and two older brother would go down to the basement where he had full photographic equipment and spend the night getting out this order, so as to have it to give to them the next day. I have visions of these postcards drying on the racks my father made – large racks on which these cards had been laid out to dry overnight."

Fanny, Willard, Ruth

LOUIS AND FANNY

An Alaskan Joins the Family

Fanny spent most of 1911 with child – her fifth. On October 5, 1911, the first true Alaskan joined the family – Willard Seward Pedersen. Family named the baby Willard in honor of Frances Willard, national president of the Women's Christian Temperance Union, in which Fanny was an activist and would later become state treasurer.

Joe Pedersen explain, "Bishop Rowe, head of all the Episcopal Church missionary work in Alaska, made it possible for Mother to have her baby in the Episcopal Church's Good Samaritan Hospital in Valdez. Seward did not have any facility other than a bed in the local doctor's home."

For a time prior to Willard's birth, "and possibly after," Joe writes, Louis hired a Chinese cook to help in the home. "He liked to bake bread and, especially, he enjoyed working the dough with his quick, skillful hands. If the dough should need more moisture, he would fill his mouth with water and, cheeks bulging, squirt water into the dough. Kneading and squirting went on until the right consistency was reached. We all lived!"

But life was about to get complicated.

Joe, Willard and Ruth dog sledding.

Seward and the 4th Street Dock. Lowell Creek is visible cutting through town diagonally. The church and Pedersen home were near the center of the photo.

Chapter 8

'Louie, Our House Is on Fire'

Guests had just finished dinner and were sitting down to look at Louis's postcards, Ruth said. It was an icy January night in 1911. Fanny started up the stairs of their home to put baby Willard to bed.

"Coming back into the living room where these guests were busy around the table with the albums, my Mother said in a very weak, little voice, 'Louie, I think our house is on fire.'

"So with that, my Dad and older brothers jumped up. Fred grabbed the extinguisher from the kitchen to go upstairs to see if he could extinguish it. Realizing it was beyond that, he turned around to come downstairs with the extinguisher still squirting.

"Out the front door went one of the tourists with Willard in her arms. It was the middle of January, the front steps were covered in ice, and she recalled afterwards how she told my Mother she would take the baby and go to the nearest house.

"Mother looked at her and the fine clothes she was wearing, because she was going to a dance afterwards – clothes including high-heeled pumps. Mother, thinking of the ice on the steps and this woman who didn't understand our weather and footing, said, 'All right but don't kill him.'

"As the woman was going down the front steps she was hit by the discharge of the fire extinguisher. She slipped and went down four steps, five steps, clutching the baby in her arms. 'I was afraid to look,' she said afterwards. 'That I when I knew what she had meant.' But nothing came of it. Neither she nor the baby was hurt."

Joe and Ruth both ran to the church half-a-bock away, where they rang the bell to summon the volunteer fire department. "I dashed out through four feet of snow to go over to the church," Ruth said. "You pulled one side of the rope for church, the other side for the fire bell. If you heard a 'dingdong, dingdong, dingdong' you knew it was fire."

Joe adds, "I ran to the church bell and rang it with all my might. Someone said, 'That is enough,' so I took off at full speed for the downtown fire bell. It was a cold, wet, sloshy night when each footstep went through the snow and was immediately engulfed in water. Little did I look where I was going, nor care. I was headed for that fire bell. My head down, I ran into a lady fair and square amidships and knocked her completely off the sidewalk into a deep pile of that cold, wet sloshy stuff. I kept on going! What did she do? I never found out."

Ruth kept on ringing the church bell. "Presently there came a hand-pulled fire hoe cart and I don't remember what other pieces of equipment. As I was pulling on that bell, one of the firemen came to me and said, 'Ruth, you can quit pulling that rope now. The firemen are here.' 'But,' I said, 'our house is still burning. You haven't got it out. I'm going to keep on ringing, and I did."

There were 13 fires in Seward that night. "It seemed the very atmosphere was just right," Joe said. "Everybody burned wet wood, and creosote buildup was heavy."

The fire gutted the attic and upstairs, Joe said. "Downstairs, the loss was by smoke and water. Dad was mainly concerned about the photographic equipment down in the basement.

"The hotel gave us rooms," he said. "Everybody lost their clothes except me. I had a room downstairs and my clothes were under the stairway."

Joe later blamed the fire on a cracked chimney flue. It was common practice in Seward to use seawater when mixing the mortar to build chimneys. This was true of the parsonage. Seawater does not bond well. This, together with the frequent shaking of Seward's many earthquakes and the heavy creosote buildup from burning wet wood provided all the elements for fire.

Yet the parsonage survived not only the 1911 fire but also the 1964 Good Friday earthquake that destroyed vast areas of Anchorage, all of Valdez and much of Seward. The parsonage was built with a log basement and log foundation that withstood the shaking.

In 1965, a year after the earthquake, Seward Memorial Methodist Church celebrated its 60th anniversary. Three Pedersen children attended – Fred, Ruth and Joe.

Joe reported in a family letter dated Oct. 20, 1965: "Fred and I slept in the home of Rev. and Mrs. Franz O. Christopher … the very same house Dad built. We had the room, which was Ruth's in the old days. A downstairs partition has been removed so that they now have a very large living room. The porch has been glassed in. It was used for a city library for a time. Some of the old log basement and foundation still shows, although the house is now on a concrete foundation.

"The back porch and steps down to the basement are still there. The same old chimney is there. People who wired the house said there is plenty of evidence of the fire in the attic. I understand this house did the rock-and-roll during the earthquake and suffered some damage, but came through well enough to be used as a shelter and refugee home for several days after the quake."

Later in 1965, after the Pedersen visit, the house burned one last time, once and for all.

Chapter 9

The Ivory Napkin Ring

Prior to Dan Pedersen's trip to Seward in 2000, Willard Pedersen mentioned an ivory napkin ring Louis gave Fanny as an anniversary gift. Dan and his wife, Sue, found it in the Seward Museum, displayed in a glass case with this card:

Anniversary gift from Rev. L.H. Pedersen to his wife Frances in 1914. Ring was carved at Dutch Harbor and acquired for Rev. Pedersen by Capt. McMullen of steamer Dora.

The napkin ring was delivered to the museum by Willard, who visited the town in 1979, intending to give the ring to the church. But he and his wife, Helen, changed their minds and later wrote a family letter explaining why.

"After church we visited the Pedersen Memorial Room adjacent to the entry hall, where pictures of Dad and Fred are displayed and some Pedersen memorabilia is on exhibit. There is an album of Dad's early-day mimeographed church bulletins, announcements of current events, YMCA lectures and socials. They are cleverly worded, illustrated with drawings and some cartoons. They clearly illustrate the very active part Dad played in the community life of Seward and very obviously are the product of a mind keenly alert, striving to better the lifestyles of people in the community. I was proud to announce he was my father. The materials there certainly confirm that in his daily contacts with others he did not short-change them.

"Ralph had asked me to deliver to the church memorial an ivory napkin ring with walrus carved on its top, given him by Dad, and I took it to the service for that purpose, together with a letter Dad had handwritten to Ralph. As I viewed the room I had misgivings. It appears to be a room by-passed by most people entering and leaving. It is not well secured against theft and I had a rather strong feeling the room was not the appropriate resting place for the valuable ivory carving. Too few people would see it. It would be too-easily slipped into someone's pocket and the loss not notice for a long time. I talked to Mrs. Mahan, a long time friend of Fred about it and her feelings were similar, only more pronounced.

Willard and Helen had visited the Seward Historical Museum in the basement of city hall and taken note of all the historical memorabilia and artifacts, including Fred's high school diploma on prominent display. "I felt this was the appropriate place for the napkin ring, among the many other artifacts, well guarded and displayed in a museum that is highly regarded and visited by most tourists."

Pedersen Glacier and Lagoon. *Fred L. Pedersen photo – 1970s.*

Chapter 10

The Family Glacier

Alfred H. Brooks, the U.S. Coast and Geodetic surveyor, will be remembered forever because the Brooks Range of northern Alaska is named for him.

Louis Pedersen will be remembered partly because Brooks named Pedersen Glacier for him.

It's an especially beautiful glacier on Pedersen Lagoon in Aialik Bay, about 10 – 12 miles southwest of Seward. Pedersen was a personal friend.

"Do I know Pedersen Glacier?" a bush pilot responded to Joe Finrow Pedersen on a visit to Seward. "I fly over it every day." The glacier has been receding for many years with at least one beneficial effect – making the lagoon at its foot even more beautiful.

Brooks led one of the first U.S. Geologic Service (USGS) field parties to Alaska after Congress appropriated the funds in 1898 for geologic and topographic surveys of the territory. He spent the rest of his career in Alaska, becoming head of Alaska Operations in 1903 and remaining in this job until his death in 1924.

Brooks almost didn't get the assignment. He was a young man in 1896 when gold was discovered in the Yukon. Congress appropriated funds to the USGS for Alaska survey work, according to USGS Fact Sheet 099-00, viewable online.

Brooks coveted an Alaska survey assignment but his chances of getting it were long, according to a colleague, Walter C. Mendenhall, who wrote this to him. "Interest here among a good many of the younger men is centered in the Alaska plans which Mr. Willis and the Director are considering … The plan being considered at present involves the sending in of four or five different parties, each in charge of a geologist and accompanied by a topographer and several camp hands. The tendency seems to be to choose pretty big men to put in charge of these parties …

"Your own application is being considered but I do not know what your chances are. I think, though, that the chance of the younger men depends in some part on the attitude of the more experienced

Pedersen Glacier when Louis Pedersen photographed it about 1908.

geologists. Several of these latter will be offered parties; if they don't want them, the boys may be given a chance."

In the end, the boys got their chance. Both Brooks and Mendenhall received Alaska assignments.

Settlement of Seward and construction of a railhead brought increased ship traffic to the Kenai Peninsula coast, along with awareness of the need for better marine surveys and navigational information. Before 1900, the charts in use dated back to Russian surveys of the 1840s. Resurrection Bay, where Seward was located, was the preeminent anchorage for ships, but the bay's entrance was hazardous because of rocky points, numerous islands, narrow passages and frequent rough weather and fog.

Brooks led at least two hydrographic and topographic surveys to the Seward area, working from the ship *S.S. McArthur* in the summers of 1906 and 1912. He surveyed the coastline from the Barren Islands to Chiswell Islands, as well as the Nuka Bay coast. Shortly after his second visit in 1912, the U.S. Coast and Geodetic Survey published a nautical chart for Aialik Bay, where Pedersen Glacier is located.

Joe Pedersen remembers Brooks as a religious man who became a warm friend of Louis and Fanny. "He would bring his boat at times to Seward where his men would have shore leave and Brooks would file his reports at the cable head.

"When at sea, Dr. Brooks conducted religious services for his men. When in port, Rev. L.H. Pedersen held special services for them.

At the time of Brooks' survey, the only way to reach Pedersen Glacier was by sea. Louis traveled there at least once with Brooks and took many photographs, which he made into post cards. Various family members later flew over the glacier with bush pilots and photographed it from the air. Willard's son, Doug, kayaked to Pedersen Lagoon and camped there. One benefit of the lagoon for campers is that grizzly bears will not cross the ice to reach the lagoon.

In 2008, the wilderness experience got a lot more civilized at Pedersen Lagoon when construction began on Kenai Fjords Glacier Lodge, a seasonal lodge with a full view of the lagoon and glacier. No doubt Louis would never have imagined there would one day be 16 cabins, electric power and a dining room, not to mention comfortable beds. His great grandson, Robert, spent a few days at the lodge in 2013, celebrating a wedding anniversary with his wife, Linda.

Because Pedersen Glacier flows down to the sea, it would be tempting to call it a tidewater glacier. Technically it isn't, because actually it flows into an upper, freshwater lagoon.

Rob said the upper lagoon was jammed full of ice at the time of his visit and he could not get across it to the face of the glacier. But he did go kayaking on the lagoon with a guide.

Rob's wife, Linda, said guests saw many Black Bears from the lodge's cabins during their stay, but none of the more formidable Grizzlies, since they won't cross the ice.

To reach the lodge, guests traveled by small boat for several hours from Seward. This was an adventure in itself, Rob said, since the boat stopped along the way to observe wildlife, and pick up and deliver kayakers to points along the coast. When they reached their destination, the boat approached the beach bow-first and they stepped ashore using a bow ramp and hiked overland about 15 minutes to the lodge, "where our suitcases were waiting for us."

Brooks party surveying Thumb Cove, Resurrection Bay. *Louis Pedersen*

Church picnic, June 27, 1913. Time to say goodbye. *Louis Pedersen photo*

Chapter 11

End of the Beginning

By the summer of 1913, Louis and Fanny knew their work in Seward was coming to an end and they'd soon move to a new assignment. It would mean saying goodbye to many friends in the town where several of their children had really grown up.

Seward had only a handful of native people, Ruth recalls. "They were mostly clustered along the beach in Indian huts that were built up on stilts. I don't think I ever was in one of those homes but I had two friends I liked so well, Amy Burns and Susie Guest.

"Amy was a half-breed girl, quiet, unassuming – I loved her very much. She was one of my favorites. The other was Susie Guest. You know, the Eskimos are of smaller stature. She was about to my shoulder and would look at you with her almost almond-shaped eyes and you'd see twinkles coming out of them. I have a picture of my birthday party and those two girls are there."

Joe Pedersen recalls a close friend of his own who is in the same picture. "Forest Vaughan and I used to hunt ptarmigan – he with his shotgun and I with my single-shot .22 target rifle. We always got four or five birds apiece."

Also in the same picture taken in the basement schoolroom of the Episcopal Church is Joe's teacher, Mrs. Tillet. "We sat on benches and had slates – yes, with the red border around the edge – and squeaky slate pencils, too.

"We saw the height of the Gold Rush to the Iditarod country. Some gold was found – a few good claims – but never enough to cause or justify a rush."

Joe recalled he got his first job selling newspapers in Seward – *The Seward Gateway*. My pay was a 2-1/2 dollar gold piece every Friday night and I was mighty proud of that money. I remember coasting down 4th Avenue, the main street, to the dock. Girls and boys, men and women, rich and poor – all were there. It was just plain fun."

Joe and Ruth grew quite close in Seward and later Skagway. "Fred and Ralph always played together. Thus, Ruth became my steadfast friend and pal."

Fanny formed close friendships, as well. Ruth recalls there was no Russian Orthodox Church in Seward but the Russian influence was evident. One of her mother's closest friends was a Russian lady, Mrs. Korth, who had been part of the Russian occupation.

Ruth's birthday March 1913: From left in back: Joe, Margaret Romig, Forest Vaughan, Mrs. Tillet, Elizabeth Romig. *Foreground:* Fanny, Blanche Dakin, Amy Burns, Ruth, Susie Guest, Thelma Ellsworth, Mary Harmon.

"She and Mother formed an intimate friendship. Once a week they would have tea together. Mother was not a tea drinker but she looked forward to these little afternoon social times together. There were several children – the one I remember chiefly was Peter. There was also Eunice Korth and Esther Korth – all raised in the Russian tradition. Mrs. Korth had a samovar she used to make tea. To go into their home was quite an experience because they had so many of the original Russian – I don't know, not antiques but choice pieces of China and accessories. They were lovely people."

In a 1976 Christmas memoir to his family, Joe Pedersen shared these impressions of his childhood. "The mountains across Resurrection Bay from Seward were of exceptional beauty. We saw them every day from our dining room window – beautiful, majestic, inspiring. We were in Seward during the early stages of what is now called the Alaska Government Railroad. When the Ballaine brothers laid out the town and started to build the railroad they called it the Alaska Central. About 1910 or 1911, the Guggenheim interests bought the railroad and named it the Alaska Northern."

Willard recalls, "One thing that impressed me about Dad was that here was a man who went up to Alaska in the very early days. I don't know what Dad's formal education was but I don't think it was much. He accumulated, somewhere along the line, a vast collection of books – good books. He had a big library in Seward and Skagway, and (later) Newhalem, Snohomish and Bellingham. He had books on literature and religion – I was always amazed. He was a good carpenter, a good photographer, a good printer when he was printing his church bulletins. I think he was a generous person. He taught school for a time when we were in Auburn."

He could also sing. Ruth recalled, "If he'd had some training he would have been quite good, but singers were scarce and far between. I've heard him sing at a church service, *Where's My Wandering Boy Tonight?* He would emote appropriately, and the women in the church sanctuary would wipe their eyes appropriately. I think it relieved tensions and created a feeling of oneness between this wandering boy and others that they didn't tell about."

Today Seward is both a railroad town and a coal port. Coal trains bring their loads from the mine at Healy, near Denali Park, for loading onto ships for Korea, where it fuels the engines of heavy industry. The coal travels south but the tourists travel north on those rails in dome cars headed for Anchorage, Denali Park and Fairbanks.

The Pedersens never got that far. They were on their way to Skagway and new adventures long before the railroad was finished.

LOUIS AND FANNY

The Family in Skagway

From left: Willard, Fanny, Ethel (Fred's wife), Joe, Fred, Ruth, Ralph, baby Andy, Louis. *Center:* Mrs. Captain J.M. Olsen (Louis's mother)

Chapter 12

War on Saloons

"Since our arrival in Alaska in 1903 we have seen gambling abolished," Fanny wrote in 1918. "(We've seen) the roulette tables removed and destroyed, sporting women prevented from frequenting saloon, the saloons closed on Sundays, the elimination of the nickel-in-the-slot machines, local Prohibition in several towns and then our goal – Prohibition throughout Alaska!

"And last and very important, many convictions and heavy fines for 'boot-legging,' and one red-light district after another closed."

Skagway is where Louis and Fanny's war on alcohol and vice really reached its peak. The Pedersens arrived in the fall of 1913, sixteen years after Skagway was founded as gateway to the Yukon gold fields in competition with nearby Dyea.

Louis took over as Methodist-Episcopal pastor of a shrinking congregation in a town that had already peaked and was in steep decline, but that still had some fight in it. Dyea disappeared entirely within a few years, but Skagway boomed as the state's largest city during in 1897 and 1898. Its population peaked at 15,000 in 1898 and then plummeted to 3,000 in 1900 and is well under 1,000 today, but the church is still there.

A big part of Skagway's sour reputation is owed to a gambler, con-man and shakedown artist named Soapy Smith, who arrived in October of 1897 and was sent to his "reward" by August of the following year in a shootout with town marshal Frank Reid, who lost his life doing it. In the 10 months of Smith's heyday, the Soapy Smith gang relieved many arriving prospectors of their goods and money before they even reached the beach. Their typical practice was to unload passengers and goods onto the tide flats at low tide and transport the loads ashore by wagon before the tide returned, which opened a window of opportunity for Smith to lend his services.

Louis's church in Skagway – still there. *Dan Pedersen photo*

LOUIS AND FANNY

Following the Alaska Purchase in 1867, the manufacture, importation, sale and distribution of liquor was strictly illegal because of the inherent danger of liquor traffic among the natives. But all efforts of the military and various federal agencies to enforce the law failed. At the height of the gold rush, some 60 saloons were operating openly, plus three breweries, Howard Clifford writes in *The Skagway Story*. "All advertised their products despite their being strictly illegal," he reports. "Nothing was done to put a stop to the manufacture or sale of alcoholic beverages." By 1899, the Prohibition had unraveled.

Mrs. S.E. Shorthill, who came to Skagway in 1897, formed the Women's Christian Temperance Union (WCTU) here in 1900, and this was to become Fanny's passion. Mrs. Shorthill led efforts to build a church and school. As a result of her activism, according to Clifford, other unions were formed and temperance speakers included Alaska on their itineraries.

Lacking the funds to enforce Prohibition, territorial governors and other officials undermined the temperance efforts by continually petitioning the President and Congress to repeal the Prohibition law, according to Clifford. This finally occurred in 1899 by a narrow margin in a vote from which more than half the House of Representatives abstained. The U.S. Senate also passed the repeal with a large number not voting.

Replacing Prohibition were "local option" laws backed by high license fees for saloons. Revenues from the high fees went to town councils, with 50 percent for the support of schools and the remainder for general use by local government. Thus, towns such as Skagway were highly dependent on liquor taxes for the construction of schools, streets and other municipal needs. The odds in local elections thus were stacked heavily in favor of a "wet" majority in any vote.

The temperance and suffrage (women's right to vote) movements in the United States were closely allied. The suffragettes employed mostly peaceful tactics in their demonstrations and political efforts, but the temperance leaders grabbed headlines with a more direct approach. A temperance sister, Carrie A. Nation, walked into a bar in Wichita, Kansas, in 1900 and smashed everything in sight with an

Serious women in front of the Presbyterian Church in Skagway are probably the territorial convention of the Alaska WCTU, which the church hosted in 1915. That's Fanny in the polka dot dress, third from left in the foreground.

axe. Over the next 10 years she did this again in some 30 more drinking establishments.

Fanny already had been active in the WCTU for several years. In Seward in 1908 she formed a close friendship with Mrs. Cornelia Templeton Hatcher (then Jewett), managing editor of *The Union Signal*, official organ of the national WCTU and president of the Illinois Women's Press Association.

Mrs. Jewett returned to Alaska in 1910 on the lecture circuit for the national WCTU and stayed in the Pedersen home as Fanny's guest. While in Alaska, Mrs. Jewett met and married Robert Lee Hatcher, a sourdough who had come to Alaska in 1896.

"She stayed in our home for several weeks," Fanny's daughter Ruth said, "and because of Mother's affiliation (with the WCTU and suffrage movements), my next brother was named Willard, after Frances Willard. Because of that, two little souvenirs were sent to my Mother from Frances Willard's home in, I believe, Evanston, Illinois. There was a little sugar shell, a very dainty one in the shape of an oak leaf bowl, and I think the other item was a butter knife. They're from the home and collection of Frances Willard. Of course they are now in my brother's possession."

In Skagway, Mrs. Shorthill's daughter, Mrs. L.A. Harrison, was now treasurer of the WCTU's local chapter. Mrs. Shorthill herself had gone on to an influential role as secretary to the Governor. Fanny was by this time treasurer of the Alaska Territorial union.

The stage was set for a new step to mount pressure against the saloons by holding a territorial convention, and what better place to do it than Skagway?

So in 1915, Louis and Fanny, and The Skagway Methodist-Episcopal Church, hosted the first Alaska Territorial Convention of the WCTU, May 13-16. Clifford reports, "The program . . . was led off with a parade of school children carrying flags and banners throughout the town." Fourteen voting delegates and followers attended from throughout the territory of Alaska. The highlight was an appearance by Mrs. Hatcher, now president of the Alaska WCTU.

Alaska WCTU officers at national convention in Seattle in 1915:

Fanny (left), Mrs. Cornelia Templeton Hatcher; Mrs. Lulu B. Thomson, Mrs. Lucy Record Spaeth; Mrs. Clara Michener.

Temperance was becoming the hottest topic of conversation everywhere in the United States, including Alaska. Following the territorial convention in Skagway, Fanny and her fellow Alaska officers traveled to Seattle for the national convention in 1915. The effort was rewarded, Howard Clifford reports. "In 1915, the Territorial legislature passed a resolution calling for a vote on a bill entitled, 'An Act providing for an expression by the people of the Territory of Alaska as to whether or not intoxicating liquors shall be manufactured or sold in the Territory of Alaska after the first of January 1918.'"

In the general election of 1916, "to the great surprise of many, prohibition was voted by an overwhelming 9,052 'dry' votes to 4,814 'wet' votes, despite a majority of the communities having voted wet in the local open elections just the preceding year."

Congress backed up the Alaskans' "expression" on Feb. 14, 1917, with an act prohibiting the manufacture or sale of liquor in Alaska. This, Clifford says, became known as the Alaska Bone Dry Law.

In 1920, the suffrage and temperance movements celebrated twin national victories. In January, Prohibition went into effect under the 18th Amendment to the Constitution. In August, women in America gained the right to vote. Fanny and women like her shared a moment of triumph.

Louis's Switch from Methodist to Presbyterian

In Skagway, Louis and Fanny took over an established church with a good building that is still standing. But those who know Skagway will note it is today called the First Presbyterian Church, not the First Methodist. It was Methodist when Louis arrived and Presbyterian when he left, and so was he. This transformation came about in a bizarre way, and it helps to know the history leading up to it.

The Russians sold Alaska to the United States in 1867, and 10 years passed before Protestant missionaries ventured north. The Presbyterians were the first, establishing a foothold in Fort Wrangell, where the minister S. Hall Young gave a damning assessment of Caucasian treatment of the native population. ". . .The most vicious, degraded, ruined and hopeless savages I have ever met in Alaska were educated white men from refined homes . . . There was something wanting in the character of these men, something weak, something ignoble."

He went on, "The moral conditions . . . were indescribably bad . . . The soldiers had done them little good and much evil. The town is full of half-breed children. The most loathsome of diseases was universally prevalent . . . Many of the poor little ones came into the world covered with scales and most of the babies died."

He described polygamy, slavery, drunkenness and constant immorality.

So it's not surprising the Louis and Fanny were consumed with the war against alcohol as the root of all evil for its impact on both natives and whites. Aside from liquor's role in a host of vices prevalent among white people, traders had supplied some native villages enough alcohol to eradicate entire populations and destroy the subsistence lifestyle in a single winter.

In fact the intensity of the family heritage on this point is so great that no alcohol was ever consumed at any family gathering for decades after Louis and Fanny died, to the author's recollection. Only much later did the occasional, social glass of wine begin to appear at the tables of grandchildren and great grandchildren.

The horrific conditions the Presbyterians found in Alaska led the legendary Alaska missionary, Dr. Sheldon Jackson, to establish the first Presbyterian Alaska mission in Fort Wrangell in 1877. By 1884, the Presbyterians had expanded to six Alaska missions staffed by seven missionaries. The Methodists, including Louis H. Pedersen, would not reach the same strength till 20 years later.

Jackson felt it would do no good for Protestant missionaries to compete against one another in the same communities, so he proposed a creative solution – a Comity Agreement with Baptists, Methodists and Episcopalians – under which they would divvy up local communities among them and rotate assignments.

The Skagway Daily Alaskan of March 29, 1917, explains.

Three years ago the Presbyterian, Episcopal and Methodist churches asked one church to send a minister to Skagway for three years. The Methodist Episcopal Church did (Louis Pedersen), ending September 30th last. Members of the Presbytery came last summer and recommended that the Presbyterian Church start out on October 1. That was done, and Mr. Pedersen continuing as the minister one year.

Another article dated Aug. 1, 1917 reports:

Since the start of the Presbyterian Church last October, Rev. L.H. Pedersen has continued at the unanimous request of the members. Now is the time to cement the relationship . . . Mr. Pedersen having signified his willingness to enter the Presbyterian Church and be received into the Presbytery of Alaska, the elders have called a meeting of the Congregation in order that the financial arrangements can be perfected.

So on September 26, 1917, Louis was inducted into the Presbytery as local pastor – changed his denomination to remain with the Skagway congregation.

Methodist historians Bea Shepard and Claudia Kelsey were a bit awed by this, writing in 1986: *In a move which we have not been able to fully comprehend, but evidently arranged by the Alaskan leaders of the Presbyterian, Episcopal and Methodist denominations, (Louis Pedersen) became the Presbyterian minister in Skagway, preaching in the same church and living in the same parsonage as he had during the previous three years. And since October 1, 1916, the church in Skagway, which had been the Methodist Episcopal Church, has been the Presbyterian Church.*

During the Skagway years, Louis was active in the Arctic Brotherhood, a fraternal organization. One of the nearby mountains at Skagway is clearly branded with large letters as A-B Mountain, and the brand was adopted as the organization's symbol. "In the spring when the snow melted it always left the outline of these two letters plainly visible on the mountainside," Ruth said.

One of the most distinctive buildings in Skagway is the old Arctic Brotherhood Hall on Broadway and Second Avenue. It is now the Seward Museum, known for its collection of Skagway artifacts, memorabilia, photography and historical records. The building's façade is comprised entirely of driftwood. The AB Skagway hall was the first camp or lodge hall of the Arctic Brotherhood in the state and Louis's son, Joe, was a member.

Another son, Willard, adds, "Dad was quite a hiker and outdoorsman. He used to do quite a bit of mountain climbing on the hills around there and I know he led many parties to the top of A-B Mountain.

LOUIS AND FANNY

White Pass and Yukon Railroad locomotive roars past Pedersen Brothers Photography in this old postcard Joe and Grace Pedersen found when they visited Skagway. Note the Pedersen Brothers sandwich board at left.

Joe adds, "I've climbed to the top of Mount Dewey and A-B Mountain. I used to hike the trails to lower Lake Dewey, upper Lake Dewey, Bear Glacier, Smugglers Cove and Black Lake on the old White Pass Trail to the Klondike. Our Alpine Club, as well as our Sunday school, conducted organized train excursions to the now world famous Lake Bennett."

Joe said he had his first automobile ride in Skagway and his first full-time job in the shops of the White Pass & Yukon Railroad. "I had two bikes and delivered the *Skagway Daily Alaskan*. Good pay, too."

Pedersen Brothers Photography

The photography business Louis started in Seward really came into its own in Skagway. The older Pedersen children were growing into adulthood, attending university, and assuming their own places in the community. Joe Pedersen recalls, "Dad, Fred, Ralph and I had a photo store in downtown Skagway, Pedersen Brothers Photography, where we sold post cards and did developing and printing mainly for the tourist trade." Later the business became "The Pedersen Company," with Fred Pedersen as manager.

Joe's son, Joe Finrow Pedersen, and his wife pinpointed the location when they visited Skagway in 1998. Guided by an old postcard taken in front of the building, they traced it to one of Skagway's original, historic buildings known (in 1998) as Moe's Frontier Bar.

"Pedersen Brothers" – Ralph, Joe, Fred

Joe Turner Pedersen continues, "Dad's postcards were excellent and we sold them wholesale to other stores up and down the Alaska coastline. Money from the venture helped to keep Ralph and Fred in school at the University of Washington."

An article in the Skagway Daily News dated March 6, 1917, reports, *Fred Pedersen and wife, according to advice received in this city on one of the last mail steamers, will return to the north on the 17th of this month and take up residence here for the summer. Mr. Pedersen will take charge of the photographic dark room of Pedersen Brothers, and it is the intention of Pedersen Brothers to vacate the small building just south of the Presbyterian Church as a workroom and move into the second story of their store building on Broadway. Mr. and Mrs. Fred Pedersen will reside in the cottage thus vacated, which will be put in shape for them shortly after their arrival here.*

Details about everyday life in the Pedersen home are revealed in newspaper articles that Ralph's son, Richard F. Pedersen, obtained from *The Skagway Daily Alaskan* from 1917-18, the year Ralph was editor. One tells of Ralph's arrival in Skagway Oct. 14, 1916, on the Canadian Pacific steamer *Alice*, after a trip to Seattle. Many ships carried passengers back and forth to Alaska in those days and the Pedersens traveled on many familiar vessels of that era, and photographed them.

LOUIS AND FANNY

Ralph Edits *The Skagway Daily Alaskan*

In July of 1917, Louis's son, Ralph, became editor of *The Skagway Daily Alaskan*. The newspaper reported he took hold of his new responsibilities "with characteristic energy and thoroughness." He brought to the job 14 years of experience in Alaska, "with the exception of the winter months, during which he was pursuing his studies at the University of Washington in Seattle."

The newspaper went on to say that at the university, Ralph completed the "special course in journalism."

Aside from being a natural writer he has had considerable experience in the mechanical production of a newspaper, having been employed in the printing departments of several newspapers in the towns in which he has resided.

Joe Runs Away to Seattle

High school did not entirely agree with Joe and he developed an attitude that escalated out of control. "I must have been a junior," he recalled in a family letter in 1978. "There were only eight in the entire high school when I took Latin. We were declining the Latin verb, 'amo" and I got as far as, "amo, amos, amet, a maw moose and a paw moose." The room went dead silent.

"After a few embarrassing moments I walked out the door and went home. I steered clear of Dad until the next day. He knew I was in trouble and I expected more trouble, too, so I looked him straight in the eye and said, 'Dad, I want to go to Seattle.' His answer was quick and very agreeable – just about knocked me off my feet. 'Ok, let's go down and buy your ticket.'"

Joe's teacher harbored no ill will. "Who do you suppose came down to the dock to wish me bon voyage? And who stood there waving her kerchief as long as I could see her? You guessed it – my Latin teacher, Miss Garrett." It was not the last Joe would see of her. She turned up years later at Washington State University, still encouraging Joe to work hard in his studies.

Joe lived for a time in the downtown YMCA in Seattle and soon landed a job at the original Boeing plant on the Duwamish waterway, soldering turnbuckles to guy wires. "That was in the day when airplanes were made of a wooden frame, fabric covering, struts and guy wires." Boeing had just 200 employees. Later, he left Boeing for better pay at the Foundation Shipyard in Tacoma, building wooden sailing ships with auxiliary steam power for the French government.

Back in Skagway, an article published in the newspaper of March 22, 1918, gives a glimpse of life in the Pedersen home.

On Thursday a delightful family gathering took place in the Manse, the occasion being the birthday of Ruth, daughter of the Rev. and Mrs. L.H. Pedersen. No one was present except the relatives and Miss Frances Kennedy, a close friend of Miss Pedersen, Mrs. Andrew Stevenson and her little daughter. Ruth contributed to the feast of good things by baking a fine birthday cake handsomely decorated with an appropriate inscription and candles. Along with the cake was given a goodly-sized freezer full of ice cream. This is the sixteenth birthday of Miss Ruth Pedersen and all her many friends are wishing her sixteen year measures of happiness.

With Joe away in Seattle, the family carried on its usual routines. On July 15, 1918, the newspaper reported:

The Skagway Alpine Club chartered a train to Bennett, B.C. in about 1917, where Louis photographed them.

LOUIS AND FANNY

Rev. and Mrs. L.H. Pedersen went to Denver Glacier this morning. They are escorting a party of tourists who will spend the day there. Mr. Pedersen says the trail is in very good shape this year, and that if a couple of days work was done in the way of cutting the high grass and trimming out some of the branches that overhang the path, it would make a good trail and many would take advantage of the fine weather to go out to the glacier. It is up to the Commercial Club to look into this matter.

In Seattle, Joe was having the time of his life. The Aug. 18, 1918 newspaper published an excerpt of a letter he sent home.

Well, how is Skagway? I hope it is still on the map. I don't care if it isn't. They cannot take it off the earth, so I am going back someday just because it is Skagway. I suppose you would like to know what I'm doing. I'm just building ships. It's my old trade. I began when I was old enough to handle a jack knife and run away from home. These boats are built on the same lines as the Pal Pyra, have five masts and a bowsprit, double funnels, double engines, twin screws. They're both steam and sail, have electric lights and wireless, two anti-submarine guns, one forward and one aft. Every chest in the yard (4,000 of them) swells with pride as one goes steaming past and they all give three cheers and the vessel answers with three toots. These vessels will all go to the French government.

"My old trade" was big talk for a teenager, but clearly, Joe had outgrown Skagway.

Louis Travels Outside for His Mother

By the time Joe wrote that letter, life was getting complicated for the family in Skagway.

In May of 1917, Louis had traveled to Astoria on the *SS Spokane* to bring his mother back to Skagway to live. "It is the first time he has been outside in seven years," the newspaper reported. "Instead of taking a long vacation as he had planned to do, he will return about June 1 to resume the duties that attend him here. His mother will come with him, to make her home here."

The reference to a long vacation hints that Louis or his family wanted or needed a break, but there was none. Upon his return with Grandma Olsen, she apparently made her home in Skagway for less than two months. On July 28, the newspaper reported, "Mrs. J.M.

Olsen . . . will return to her home in Astoria on the *Sophia*, sailing Monday night."

Adding to the confusion about Mrs. Olsen's plans, the Dec. 29, 1917 newspaper reports that the Pedersens gathered all their Skagway relatives under the roof on Christmas Day for a family reunion. Those present included "Mrs. Captain Olsen, mother of Mr. Pedersen."

It must have been quite a Christmas because the temperature was 25 to 30 degrees below zero on Christmas Day – the coldest weather on record in Skagway.

By this time, both the world situation and the family situation had taken unsettling turns. In April of 1917 the United States entered World War I, declaring war against Germany. By May 1, a contingent of "Home Guards" had been organized in Skagway to protect against saboteurs and spies. Among the 76 Skagway men who signed up were Louis, Fred and Ralph Pedersen.

Tuberculosis

Several of the newspaper articles Richard Pedersen discovered indicate multiple health problems in the family. In June 1917, Dick's father, Ralph, traveled to Seattle to see a specialist after a severe attack of pleurisy. In time it would become clear this was actually tuberculosis.

The oldest son, Fred, was now a Methodist minister in Pe Ell, Washington. He contracted typhoid fever early in 1917 and landed in Seattle General Hospital. He spent much of that winter confined to his room with the illness and gave up his position as pastor to return to Skagway with his wife, Ethel, to focus on his own recovery. In Skagway he took charge of the family photography business.

Joe had run away to Seattle in the spring of 1918. Louis's mother apparently didn't care for Skagway, either. Ruth recalls that Grandma Olsen was not used to children and the household disruption caused by the stream of visitors to the minister's home. Thanks to the Comity Agreement, Louis had the use of two houses – the Presbyterian manse and the tiny Methodist parsonage next door.

"Dad had set up his study and office over there," Ruth said, "in the Methodist parsonage. After Grandmother had been with us for a while in the manse, it became evident she would be happier by herself. So the folks fixed her up over there and she was very comfortable."

In addition to Ralph and Fred's serious illnesses, Ruth also was having health problems. An article in the June 22, 1918 newspaper reports that Fanny, Ruth, Willard and Andy had gone on vacation to the neighboring town of Haines, and returned to Skagway "now that Ruth has regained her health."

Louis and Fanny must already have been thinking about pulling out of Skagway.

They must have hoped that a long vacation and a different climate would enable them to return to their Alaska work refreshed at some future time. On July 20, 1918, the newspaper reported curiously, "The Rev. L.H. Pedersen will move his family to Tacoma the latter part of August and devote a year to manual labor, taking a rest from his chosen work as minister."

Three weeks later, the newspaper reported a different plan. A going away reception was given for Fanny by leaders of the WCTU, who "bid her good by and success in her new home in Nevada, where she and her family will go at the end of the present month."

Two weeks after that, Aug. 12, 1918, the newspaper states:

Rev. Pedersen and family will leave on the Prince Rupert on Saturday, Aug. 31, and after spending a few weeks with friends in Seattle and Tacoma, proceed to some place in Nevada where they will remain for some time to come. Nevada has been selected as a place of residence owing to the damp climate along the coast, and it is deemed more helpful to various members of the family.

But they never went to Nevada. They had tickets for a late-October departure on the *Princess Sophia* looking forward to anywhere but Alaska.

Princess Sophia "safely" aground on Vanderbilt Reef on the morning of Oct. 25, 1918. Note stiff wind blows the smoke from the ship's stack straight out.
P87-1705 Alaska State Library Winter & Pond Photo Collection. Published with permission.

Chapter 13

The Sophia Disaster

The elegant Canadian Pacific pocket liner, *Princess Sophia*, left Skagway with 353 souls aboard on October 23, 1918, bound for Seattle.

Hours later, in a snowstorm, it ran hard aground Vanderbilt Reef, near Juneau.

Things weren't too bad. Despite the rough impact, all aboard were safe and relatively comfortable. They were almost within sight of Juneau. The ship still had electrical power and normal services.

"She was sitting high on the reef, apparently safe," Willard Pedersen reports. "Some smaller ships came close by offering to take some of the passengers. The story was the captain wouldn't let the passengers go because he thought it wasn't safe for them to do so. Also, another Canadian-line vessel was to arrive the next day to take the passengers. The skipper decided not to let anyone off."

That cautious decision cost everyone their lives.

"During the night a heavier storm came up," Willard said. "The ship shifted off the reef and sank, and everyone was lost." Vanderbilt Reef is the top of an underwater mountain that rises about 1,000 feet from the bottom of Lynn Canal.

By sheer luck, no Pedersens were aboard.

Agents for the company had asked the Pedersen family to move up their travels one week earlier, which they did.

"The reason for moving up our departure one trip earlier was because a large party of miners were coming out of Canada," Ruth said. "They had completed their summer's work and had asked to take over the ship for that particular trip. The local authorities asked our folks if they would mind moving up one trip.

Many members of the Pedersen family traveled to and from Skagway on the *Sophia* over the years. Fred and Ethel Pedersen arrived in Skagway March 17, 1917, on the *Sophia*. On June 4, Louis and his mother arrived on it. On July 30, Mrs. Olsen returned to Astoria on it. But on that all-important day in 1918, they had changed their plans.

The Pedersens left Alaska in a hurry, their plans changing day to day as they responded to developing health crises in the family, of which Ralph's tuberculosis was paramount. They did not take a vacation. Louis did not take a furlough from the ministry for a year to do manual labor. They did not move to Nevada. Nor Tacoma. Nor even New Mexico.

"Ralph returned to Seattle in 1918," Joe reports. "He engaged in newspaper work until he suffered a relapse and again had to return to the hospital, this time in Albuquerque, New Mexico. After a long period of recuperation he became business secretary of the YMCA in

Miami, Arizona, and in August 1922 was married to Gertrude May Foote. They lived their early married years in the Southwest."

Family and some of the family lived temporarily in Ellisport, on Vashon Island, while Louis looked for a home for them. Joe remained in Tacoma, a short ferryboat ride away, working in the shipyard and visiting home on weekends.

In late summer of 1919 the entire family settled in the Rainier Valley of Seattle. Louis became camp secretary of the Army YMCA at Fort Stevens, Oregon. Ruth and Joe enrolled in Seattle's Franklin High School.

Early in 1919, Ruth and Joe suffered severe attacks of the Spanish Influenza, the deadliest flu the world had ever known. "After some periods of very heavy bleeding we began to improve," Joe wrote. "Thanks to our lady doctor we made good recoveries."

Ruth recalls her mother cared for almost the entire family during the flu epidemic.

"Six of us came down with the flu at one time – five kids and the grandmother. Mother was the only one who was not down with the flu. She went from one sick person to another, taking care. We were all quite ill. She was up day and night looking after us. Finally her older sister came from Raymond to stay with us."

Back: Ruth, Joe, Ethel *(Fred's wife)*, Ralph, Mother Marion *(Louis's second wife)*, Gertrude *(Ralph's wife)*, Fred, Louis, Dorothy. *Front:* Mrs. Captain Olsen *(Louis's mother)*, with two boys, likely Andy and Willard.

Chapter 14

Fanny's Death

Within a year, Fanny was dead.

She died April 10, 1920 at age 49-1/2 from a blood clot on the brain. Joe Pedersen's handwritten notes indicate her death followed two surgical operations for removal of a tumor in her womb.

"Her passing had a tremendous effect on me. I was shocked beyond words when I saw her lying in the casket. She was 50. I was 20."

Almost exactly a year later, on April 15, 1921, Louis moved with Ruth, Willard, Andy and Joe to the Skagit Electrical Project at Newhalem, Washington, where he became the welfare worker in charge of all recreational and religious work.

Ten days after the move, Louis married Ada Marion Holt in Auburn. She was a member of White River Presbyterian Church in Auburn, where Louis was serving as minister, a close friend of the Pedersen family, and of Fanny.

Fred, Louis, Willard, Joe, Andy

"She became Mother Marion in our home," Joe writes, "and quickly won a place in our hearts." Louis and Marion's only child, Dorothy, was born a year-and-a-half later, Dec. 14, 1922.

In later years, Louis enjoyed projects in his woodshop.

Life in the Pedersen home was complicated. The younger children were still in shock and grieving at the death of their mother. No one could take her place in their lives, no matter how hard their new stepmother tried. Now there was a new baby, Dorothy, and a senile grandmother, Mrs. Olsen. Each member of the household adjusted as best they could.

Mrs. Olsen's senility was an increasing problem. Her confusion posed a danger not only to herself but to the family's safety as well. Ruth, by this time, was in charge of the household, including meals. She said of Mrs. Olsen, "After Mother died (Grandma Olsen) wanted to help me, and she meant it. But she was just as confused as she could be." Several emergencies ensued in the home involving accidents that nearly led to fire or other disasters, such as placing all the household's silver flatware in the oven and melting it!

Louis reluctantly took his mother to Northern State Hospital in Sedro-Woolley, a mental institution, where she lived a short time until her death in 1926.

Following his work on the Skagit Electrical Project at Newhalem, Louis went on to new pastorates in Snohomish in 1924 and later in Concrete, Washington. He served his final years of ministry in Bellingham, where he was the first pastor of Birchwood Community Church, beginning in May of 1931 and continuing until his death on January 27, 1939.

Sometime before his death, Louis typed a short poem on his old Smith-Corona portable typewriter. The yellowed scrap would be easy to miss in the pile of papers, notes, clippings and ideas he saved. But its meaning is unmistakable.

Shadows

Once more I sit at evening

And watch the embers burn

The shadows all come creeping

Around me as I turn.

And then I see a sweet face
From which all care is gone,
That starts my soul to dreaming
Of old times, love and song.

I know you're 'way off yonder
But still you seem with me;
And in the evening shadows,
Your form I almost see.

I almost hear you whisper,
These words "I love but you,
And soon we'll be united
Sweetheart, be brave, be true."

Louis in his study, with his old Smith Corona typewriter.

Epilogue

'Be Useful. Then You Should Be Happy'

Some of Louis and Fanny's accomplishments are easy to quantify – the church they founded in Seward, the congregations they nurtured in Douglas and Skagway, the YMCA they brought to Seward, their work for temperance and suffrage, and the photographic record they created of frontier life in Alaska.

Other accomplishments perhaps are less obvious but just as important – the example of their lives, their championing of books and reading, their progressive thinking and social advocacy, promotion of schools, libraries and other civic institutions, thousands of acts of kindness and compassion, and their appeal to the fundamental goodness and humanity of each person they met.

Acts of kindness and encouragement are gifts that trickle down in the human spirit and in family culture. It is not hard to imagine that somewhere tonight, someone's life is better because their grandfather was touched by Louis's kindness and resolved to live better. Something happened to their grandfather a century ago at a remote campsite in the mountains of Alaska.

A tall figure emerged from the trail and approached this prospector at his wilderness claim. The visitor introduced himself and offered a loaf of bread his wife had baked. And then they sat down at the campfire and talked – broke the spell of loneliness with some philosophy, jokes and companionship. The visitor offered warm words of encouragement and invited the sourdough to visit his own home and his church when he came down from the mountains to Seward in a few months.

It was something the visitor didn't have to do but it was his nature. The miner knew it. Louis helped him feel part of something greater than this empty wilderness – part of a community that cared about him, and he never forgot it.

Together, with Mother Marion's help after Fanny's death, Louis and Fanny raised seven children who went on to careers of service in the ministry, in law and journalism, the medical field, business and teaching. Five of the seven, including Dorothy, raised families of their own, as did many of their children's children.

Writing in 1911 to congratulate Fanny's brother Frank and his new bride Clara on their marriage, Louis said something revealing.

"I hope both of you will find in married life the happiness you anticipate. The one who lives alone, from choice, lives less than half the possible life. Each needs the other to bring out his best. Of course, all of us want happiness, yet it is a question if that should be the goal of sensible people." Instead of happiness, he suggested, "It should possibly be *usefulness*. If one is useful, he should be happy."

Every family has a culture. Louis and Fanny, and Marion, came from pioneer stock and raised their children to be self-reliant and strong, to build, to serve and to be useful. Fred, their oldest son and later patriarch of the extended family, once remarked at a large family gathering. "Look at this family. There isn't a single Pedersen who didn't turn out well."

No Pedersens remain in Alaska, but the Last Frontier pulls family members back every few years like a magnet. If the story of the Pedersens' life in Alaska seems like ancient history to the current generation, it is not. Alaska is still there, little changed from a century ago. The Pedersen impact is still visible.

Pedersens will travel to Alaska in the years to come because we share the universal human curiosity to see where our ancestors lived and how they lived. Those who go as tourists will be enthralled by Alaska's raw power and beauty. Those who go with a sense of history will have a profoundly moving, intimate and personal experience, traveling back to the rich lives of their ancestors. They will walk in the same footsteps, behold the same wonders and experience the same emotions.

Fred, Joe, Mother Marion, Andy, Ruth, Dorothy, Willard in the 1960s.

Appendix 1
The L. H. Pedersen Family

From Joe Turner Pedersen's 1968 Research

Louis Klaus Olaus Haapstock Pedersen

Birth: Nov. 5, 1867, Steamer North Star (Norwegian flag)

Death: Jan. 27, 1939, Bellingham, Washington, buried Woodlawn Cemetery

Married: May 15, 1890, Oysterville, Washington.

Children: Seven including a daughter, Dorothy, born of his second marriage, to Ada Marion Holt.

Note: Joe Pedersen's research in 1968 was based on private papers, legal and church documents which had been preserved and were in his possession. They indicate the following line of descent:

LOUIS AND FANNY

Klaus Iverson Lokaunet (1770 – 9/22/1855) married Ingeborg (1777 – 9/11/1858). Peder's daughter

Peder Klausen Lokaunet married Karen (1800-9/22/1880), Ole's daughter of Gudbrandsdalen

Klaus Olaus Pedersen Lokaunet (6/1/1835 – 11/29/1867) married Maren Anna Groven (9/22/1849 – 1926)

Klaus Olaus Hopstock Pedersen (11/5/1867 – 1/27/1939) married Mary Fanny Turner (11/1/1870 – 4/10/1920)

The name Lokaunet, also spelled Lokovnet, seems to indicate the area or region from which the family originated. Or, it may, in a broad sense, indicate the family itself. The old country name was changed, probably when Louis Pedersen was a child in school, to Louis (pronounced Louie by Grandmother Olsen) H. Pedersen. Joe Pedersen said he can find no evidence of any legal change – it was probably just a matter of convenience. "Dad lived his life as Louis H. Pedersen."

In November 1922, Louis wrote the following: "My father ruptured a blood vessel in his heart and died when I was two weeks old." The chain of events surrounding the birth of Louis, the church steeple fall and subsequent death of his father are a little confused, but from a number of stories and a few well-confirmed facts, Joe Pedersen concluded the following:

"My father's father, Klaus Olaus Pedersen Lokaunet, was a laborer working on construction of a church steeple in the far northern city of Hammerfest, Norway, when he fell, suffering a serious internal injury. His wife, Anna, 18 years of age, was living at the home of her parents, Mr. and Mrs. Andersen Groven in Trondheim, central Norway, awaiting the arrival of her first baby. Although the baby's arrival was imminent, she decided to go to the aid of her injured husband. With very limited resources but perhaps some help from her parents, she purchased third-class passage on the coastal steamer, North Star. The boat journey took a week or more and while enroute she gave birth to a son.

News of the birth down in the steerage and the circumstances of the mother's near-destitute situation soon became known throughout the little ship. Wishing to help as best they could, the passengers and crew took up a collection and presented the new mother with a gift of silver coins.

In her joy at the birth of her son and in gratitude to the captain, passengers and crew, she included the captain's name in the name of her son and called him Klaus Olaus Hopstock Pedersen. Sometime later, Anna Pedersen engaged a silversmith to hammer out one of the coins too form a beautiful silver spoon which she kept always, in memory of the kind passengers and crew who helped her so much in her time of need.

Details of the first 2-1/2 years when they were in Norway are lacking, but when Louis was less than three years of age his mother brought him to America seeking a new start in life. They first settled in Chicago, where they were among the many thousands who had to flee for their lives in the great fire of 1870. Grandmother may have married again while in Chicago. On numerous occasions, Dad has told me of his "Stepfather Peterson," whom he remembered from his early childhood. An old tintype shows Grandmother with my father standing at her knee and another child held on her lap. Although I have no direct proof, it is reasonable to assume this child was a half-brother, Johnnie, the son of "Stepfather Peterson." Johnnie died before his first birthday, possibly as young as six months.

Not long after the Chicago fire, Grandmother Olsen, as we children knew her, moved to Astoria, Oregon, where on August 31, 1877 she married Captain Johan Martin Olsen, her third husband. How long they lived together I do not know, but Grandmother and Dad were alone for the years when he grew into young manhood. She earned a living by knitting fishnets for the Columbia River fishermen. Dad worked for the Ross Higgins Company in their butcher shop and grocery store. He later worked as secretary in the Astoria YMCA. Dad was granted his citizenship when he was honorably discharged from the Oregon State Militia, presumably about 1887 or 1888.

Dad and Mother met in Portland, Oregon, while they were students at Portland Business College. No doubt this would have been in the year or two between his militia service and their marriage in

LOUIS AND FANNY

Oysterville, Pacific County, Washington, on May 15, 1890. How often he did it, I do not know, but Dad has told me he walked the 30-mile length of Long Beach (Washington) to court Mother, who then lived in Oysterville. The first 12 years of their married life were spent in Oregon, where Dad, as a young Methodist minister, served several charges, among them Brooks, Woodburn and Silverton. In 1902, after the birth of Ruth, the fourth child, the family moved to Alaska where Dad continued his work in the Methodist Ministry at Douglas, Seward and Skagway.

The following quote from a letter Dad wrote gives so many events, names, dates and places that I wish to copy it here in its entirety:

"Ordained Deacon in Methodist Episcopal Church by Bishop Edward G. Andrews at Ashland, Oregon, September 23, 1900.

"Ordained Elder in the same church by Bishop Earl Cranston at Grants Pass, Oregon, September 28, 1902.

"Honorably dismissed from the Puget Sound Conference September 15, 1917, papers signed by Bishop M.A. Hughes and Robert C. Hartley, Secretary. Received into the Presbytery of Alaska September 25, 1917, and stationed as supply in Skagway, and later as pastor of the Presbyterian Church of that city.

"Dismissed from the Presbytery of Alaska to Presbytery of Seattle April 7, 1919. In War work as Camp Secretary of the Army YMCA until spring of 1920. Then stationed at Auburn as Stated Supply and later as pastor until appointed to this work, Skagit Electric Project, under Lumber Camp Division, Board Home Missions, here since April 15, 1921.

"Dismissed from the Presbytery of Seattle to Presbytery of Bellingham, April 20, 1921."

The family departed Alaska in 1919, took up residence in Seattle while Dad served as YMCA secretary in the Army. He was stationed at Fort Stevens, Oregon, only a short distance from his boyhood home in Astoria. At the close of World War I he returned to the pastorate, serving churches in Auburn, Newhalem, Snohomish, Concrete and Bellingham.

April 10, 1920, while Dad was pastor of the White River Presbyterian Church in Auburn, Mother passed away, leaving two youngsters and two teenagers at home and two grown sons away from home. She was buried in Mountain View Cemetery on the brow of the hill overlooking Auburn and the valley below.

April 25, 1921, Dad married Ada Marion Holt in Auburn, who quickly found her place in the hearts and lives of us all. January 27, 1939, Dad passed away in the city of Bellingham while he was still active in the Christian Ministry, to which he had given his whole life. He was buried in the forested quiet of Woodlawn Cemetery only a little way north of Bellingham, Washington.

(Signed) Joe Pedersen, November 10, 1968, Mount Vernon, Washington.

Mary Frances (Fanny) (Turner) Pedersen

Birth: Nov. 1, 1870, Stilevsville, Indiana

Death: April 10, 1920, Auburn, Washington, buried Mountain View Cemetery, Auburn

Married: May 15, 1890, Oysterville, Washington

Children: Six

Notes: Third child of Joseph Harriman Turner and Martha Ann (Brownfield) Turner. Moved at age 1 with her parents to Oregon, and one year later to Washington. Family resided in the Willapa River and Willapa Bay areas – the towns of Raymond, South Bend, Nachotta, Oysterville, Bay Center and Tokeland. At age of 20, married Louis H. Pedersen, a young Methodist minister, and moved to Oregon. During the years in Oregon when hardship and sacrifice were the rule, and the Alaska years which followed when hardship and sacrifice were multiplied, she had time to rear her family of six, to love and nurture many of the sick and needy children of the Alaska natives, to take her place among the women of the church and to be the constant companion and source of inspiration to her husband. Her death was untimely; she was not yet 50 when she passed away April 10, 1920, in Auburn, Washington.

Louis and Fanny Pedersen's Children and Their Spouses

Frederick Louis Pedersen

Birth: May 26, 1893, Astoria, Oregon

Death: June 6, 1976

Married: October 25, 1916, Seattle, Washington to Ethel Josephine LaViolette. Children: None

Notes: First child of Louis and Fanny Pedersen. Early education in grade schools of Oregon and Alaska. High school training started in Seward, Alaska, and was continued at Willamette University Prep School, and completed in Seward where he was a member of the first class to graduate from the high school in 1911. Later attended College of Puget Sound and University of Washington, from which he graduated in 1916. Later that year, he married Ethel Josephine LaViolette, a childhood friend from Juneau, Alaska days, and a church and school friend from University of Washington years. Entered the ministry following several years at Drew University and Union Theological Seminary. Served in several pastorates in Washington and became superintendent of Walla Walla District. In fall 1946 he moved to Philadelphia, where he became associate director for the Board of National Missions for the Methodist Church. Traveled extensively in U.S. doing research and developmental work for the Department of Church Extension. Because of his interest and great skill in photography, he made valuable contributions to the publications and special reports of his denomination. Awarded Doctor of Divinity Degree by the University of Puget Sound at a special convocation in 1950, in recognition of his deep devotion and untiring efforts for the church. Retired in 1963 to Tacoma, Washington, where he served part-time with the University and in Mason Methodist Church. Following the death of his wife, Ethel, in 1965, he moved to Des Moines where he served as admissi0ons consultant for the Methodist Retirement Home of Wesley Gardens and Wesley Terrace.

Ethel Josephine (LaViolette) Pedersen was born in Spokane, Washington, May 12, 1894, the first child of Frances A. and Louise LaViolette. Ethel received her early schooling in Juneau, Alaska, and in Everett and Seattle, Washington. She graduated from the University of Washington in June 1916, a member of the same class with Fred L. Pedersen, whom she married in October of that year. Changing from the role of minister's daughter to that of a minister's wife, she became intensely interested in the pipe organ and the music of the church. For years she was the official organist of the Puget Sound Conference. Her interest and activity in the church continued to intensify throughout the long period of the active ministry of her husband, until ill health forbid. Death came to Ethel December 1, 1965. Following memorial services in Mason Methodist Church, Tacoma, she was laid to rest in Mountain View Cemetery near the city of Auburn.

Ralph Martin Pedersen

Birth: August 6, 1894, Astoria, Oregon

Death: June 1, 1980

Marriage: August 12, 1922, Laguna Beach, California to Gertrude May Foote. Children: Two, Richard Foote Pedersen and Ralph Martin Pedersen Jr.

Notes: Second son. Early education in grade and high schools of Oregon and Alaska. With his older brother, Fred, he attended prep school at Willamette University in Salem, Oregon. Later attended College of Puget Sound in Tacoma and the University of Washington in Seattle. Serious illness interrupted his university work and he returned home to Skagway, Alaska, in spring of 1916. After a period of recuperation he became editor of the local daily newspaper. In 1918 he returned to Seattle, where he engaged in newspaper work until he suffered a relapse and again had to return to the hospital, this time in Albuquerque, N.M. After a long period of recuperation he became business secretary of the YMCA in Miami, Arizona. In August 1922, he was married to Gertrude May Foote. They lived their early married years in the Southwest, where he served the YMCAs in Albuquerque, N.M., and Miami, Ariz. In 1925 he became general secretary of the YMCA in Douglas, Arizona, and in 1934 he moved to Stockton, California, where he served for 19 years. His last three years of active YMCA work were in Las Vegas, Nevada. While in Stockton and again in Las Vegas, he directed fund-raising campaigns, which led to new buildings. In 1957 he retired from YMCA work, devoting part of his time each year to church, YMCA and civic interests, and to travel.

Gertrude May (Foote) Pedersen was born in Dallas, Texas, July 28, 1901, daughter of Frederick Norman Foote and Nora French (Thompson) Foote. She received her early education in Dallas, Brooklyn, N.Y., and St. Paul, Minnesota, where she graduated from Central High School. She attended the University of Washington where she met Ralph. Along with the responsibilities of the home and family she found time to be active in church, school, YMCA and civic affairs of the community. She was California Mother of the Year for 1948 and a life member of the P.T.A.

Joseph Turner Pedersen

Birth: Dec. 15, 1899, Salem, Oregon

Death: May 24, 1992, Mount Vernon, Washington

Married: June 4, 1929, Spokane, Washington to Mildred Isabel Pederson. Children: Four. Frederick T. Pedersen, Joe Finrow Pedersen, Frances E. Pedersen, Daniel M. Pedersen.

Notes: Third son. Received grade school training in Seward and Skagway, Alaska, and high school in Skagway and at Franklin High School in Seattle, graduating in 1919. During summer vacations in his later high-school years, and for four years after high school, he worked at the building trades – shipbuilding, bridge building, high-pressure water, steam and air pipe installation, air compression, and constructing residences. He notes, "In view of present developments it is interesting to note I worked for Boeing in 1919 when it was a 'rich man's hobby' employing about 200 people." In 1923 he left the building trades to continue his studies at Washington State College, receiving both his bachelor's degree and five-year Normal Diploma in 1928. In summer of 1932 he received one of the last Life Diplomas granted to teachers by the state of Washington. In June 1929, he married Mildred Isabel Pederson, to whom he had been introduced at WSC because of the similarity of names. They took up residence in Pasco, Washington, where he taught industrial arts in the high school. In 1938 the family moved to Mount Vernon where he continued his teaching career as supervisor of industrial arts. He retired in 1966 after 38 years of teaching shop classes and architectural drawing in the high school, and in college night classes.

Mildred Isabel (Pederson) Pedersen was born in Spokane, Washington, May 14, 1907, the only daughter of Martin Andrew Pederson and Caroline Anetta (Finrow) Pederson. As a little child she resided in Port Hill, Idaho, where her father was engaged in the mercantile business. Later, the family moved to Spokane where she attended grade and high schools, graduating from North Central High School in 1924. She attended Whitworth College near Spokane for two years and Washington State College in Pullman for her junior and senior years. She received her BS degree in Education from Washington State College in 1928. She taught high school chemistry in Lacrosse, Washington, for one year before her marriage in 1929. She served as church organist for most of her married life, later continuing to share her rich background and knowledge of church music through full-time teaching of organ and piano.

Ruth Frances (Pedersen) Haugen

Birth: March 28, 1902, Silverton, Oregon.

Death: February 25, 1987, Des Moines, Washington.

Married: May 23, 1926, Snohomish, Washington to Oskar Haugen. Divorced: 1933. Children: None

Notes: Born in the Methodist Parsonage in Silverton, Oregon, the fourth child and only daughter of Rev. Louis and Fanny Pedersen. It was her expected arrival that delayed the family's departure to the Alaska Mission Field. Although Ruth was a baby in Douglas, she became a young lady during the years in Seward, where she received the first five years of her grade school training. She continued grade school and started high school while in Skagway, completing her formal education in Seattle, Auburn, Bellingham and a summer session at the University of Washington in 1929. She started music lessons while a small child in Alaska and continued at an accelerated pace throughout her school days in Snohomish and Bellingham, preparing her well for a long period of teaching piano. She performed frequently as guest artist on radio and TV programs and later her own program on KIMA radio in Yakima. Illness often interrupted her teaching, and it was while she was a hospital patient she first started her work in medical records. This work continued to grow and she became a licensed medical records librarian with administrative responsibility at Yakima Valley Memorial Hospital. She also served as a consultant for other area hospitals. On May 23, 1926 she was married to Oskar Haugen, a high-rigger in the logging industry, in Snohomish, Washington. They were divorced in 1933 in Everett, Washington.

Willard Seward Pedersen

Birth: October 5, 1911, Valdez, Alaska

Death: July 14, 2007, Seattle, Washington

Marriage: July 30, 1938, Seattle, to Helen Clark Hunter. Children: One, Douglas Hunter Pedersen

Notes: Fourth son, born in Good Samaritan Hospital, Valdez, Alaska. Attended schools in Snohomish and Seattle, where he graduated from West Seattle High School in 1929. Undergraduate and graduate work at University of Washington, where he received his AB degree in 1933 and an LLB in 1935. For five years he was engaged in private legal practice in Seattle, followed by a four-year term of service in the US Navy, where he was affiliated with the Office of Naval Intelligence. Much of his service was in Southeastern Alaska, the area in which he had lived as a boy. Honorably discharged from the Navy in October 1945, as a lieutenant commander. In 1945, received his LLM degree from the University of Michigan, whereupon he began his career on the legal staff of The General Insurance Company of America, later SAFECO. In 1938, married Helen Hunter, a classmate from high school and university days. They have one son, Douglas.

Helen Clark (Hunter) Pedersen was born October 15, 1910, in Miles City, Montana, daughter of Frank Hunter and Mabel Clark Hunter. She received her early schooling in Miles City and her high school education in West Seattle, where she graduated in 1929. She received her BA in music from the University of Washington in 1933 and her teaching certificate one year later. She taught music in Wrangell, Alaska and in Ann Arbor, Michigan, and is founder and past director of the Haller Lake Methodist Church High School Choir.

Andrew Groven Pedersen

Birth: June 14, 1916, Skagway, Alaska

Marriage: March 27, 1936 Stockton, California, to Elsie Maxine Wallis. Children: Two, Nancy Ruth Pedersen and Andrew James Pedersen

Notes: Fifth son, but sixth child. Born on Flag Day, June 14, 1916, in White Pass Hospital in Skagway, 18 years too late for the gold rush that had brought worldwide fame to the now nearly deserted town. Curiously, Andrew went on to become a very successful businessman in the manufacture and sale of what he called "pounded gold jewelry." At the age of two he moved with his family to Washington, where he attended schools in Concrete, Snohomish and Bellingham. He graduated from Bellingham High School in 1935. The next year he moved to California to live with his brother, Ralph, in Stockton. In March 1936 he married Elsie Maxine Wallis. Andy served in the Merchant Marine from 1943 to 1945, his travels taking him to Tasmania, the Solomon Islands, Australia, India and Ceylon. From 1945 – 1946 he served in the U.S. Navy, based at San Diego. His flair for salesmanship brought him rapid advancement in San Francisco stores and later led him into the manufacturing and selling of gold and plastic jewelry. The selling of insurance finally became the vocation to which he devoted his life and talents.

Elsie Maxine (Wallis) Pedersen was born August 9, 1916, in Caldwell, Idaho, the daughter of Edward Wallis and Ethel Moudy Wallis. She received her elementary education in the schools of Walla Walla, Washington and Modesto, California. She attended high schools in Modesto and Stockton, from which she was graduated in 1934. She was active in the Glee Club at school and in the Epworth League of her church. During the years when her family was growing up she took a very active role in Girl Scouts and Cub Scouts. She later became active in lodge work and, along with her husband, in folk dancing.

Dorothy Marion (Pedersen) Vogel

Born after Louis remarried Ada Marion (Holt) Pedersen, following Fanny's death,

Birth: December 16, 1922, Auburn, Washington

Marriage: May 10, 1952, Spokane, Washington, to Owen Alfred Vogel. Children: Two. Janis Marion Vogel and Judith Margaret Vogel.

Notes: Daughter of Louis H. Pedersen and Ada Marion (Holt) Pedersen. Received her early education in the grade and high schools of Concrete and Bellingham, Washington, graduating from Bellingham High School in 1940. Attended Western Washington College of Education and took nurse training at St. Joseph's Hospital in Bellingham, where she received her RN degree in 1943. From 1944 to 1946 she was a first lieutenant in the Army Nursing Corps, serving first at Fort Lewis, Washington and later at Rouen and Marseilles, France. After the signing of the Armistice, she was returned to the U.S., where she served at Gardner Hospital in Chicago, doing some work among disabled veterans. Following her discharge from the Army, she attended the University of Washington, graduating in 1948 with a BS degree in Public Health Nursing. She was employed as a public health nurse in the Spokane city health department and in the Veterans Administration Hospital in Spokane. In 1952 she was married to Owen Vogel, supervisor of plant services for the Bonneville Power Administration. Rev. Fred L. Pedersen officiated. After devoting 12 years raising a young family in the home, she returned to the field of public health, serving as coordinator for the new Home Health Services program in Spokane County Health Department.

Owen Vogel was born in Gallup, N.M., November 12, 1913, the son of Orville A. Vogel and Sarah Cochran Vogel. A hunter and fisherman with great love of the outdoors, he traveled far and wide throughout the Pacific Northwest and Alaska. He was an administrator for the Bonneville Power Authority.

Appendix 2

Joseph Turner Pedersen Interview
1899-1992
Interviewed 4-15-1978 by Lisa Pedersen, his daughter-in-law
Transcribed 11-8-2000 by Dan Pedersen, his youngest son

This is Joe Pedersen, the third son of Rev. Louis H. Pedersen, missionary to Alaska roughly from the year 1902 to 1918. Dad was a young Methodist minister in Oregon. He had served two or three charges as they were then called and had made application to become a missionary thinking that perhaps that they would be sent to Africa.

DOUGLAS, ALASKA: 1902-1905

There was no available opening at the time so, more or less, Dad and Mother were waiting. Mother was expecting my sister (Ruth) in the very near future so the waiting had a dual purpose. During that waiting period the bishop informed Dad that he had nothing in Africa but that there was an opening coming in Alaska and would they consider it. Dad and mother talked it over and said yes and informed the bishop but said they would like to wait until after the arrival of the baby. So in about June of 1092, after Ruth was born, they departed Seattle to go to the then thriving mining town of Douglas, Alaska. There were several mines in Douglas. Some of them were an open-pit type of mine. Across the channel and on the hillside was a tremendous big mine at Thane. A great many people of foreign nationality had been hired by the mining companies and it was to these people that Dad was sent as a missionary.

Our steamboat let us off in Juneau. We had to get across the Gastineau Channel to the town of Douglas and that was accomplished by a small launch. I was at that time between two and three years of age – pretty small to remember much. But in the two-year time that we were in Douglas a few things do stand out in my mind. I can remember going with Dad to see what's called The Glory Hole – a tremendous big open-pit mine. And there, down in the bottom of the Glory Hole, we could see these spider-like things moving around and they were men, working way down there. And that rock was picked up, lifted out and taken to the stamping mill, which broke the rock up and got the gold out of it. But as a little youngster it impressed me very much.

There were other mines. Some of them had gone down quite deeply in the earth and had turned to follow the gold vein under the channel, and actually they were under the saltwater. And men were working down I would say pretty near a mile in the earth down there.

Some of the hardships that I know the folks had to endure in Douglas were the hardships of the severe cold and the long, drawn-out winters. I remember the great fear of fire – adults and children alike suffered from that fear and it was doubtless well founded because often the fire hydrants were frozen when a fire would break out. Who knew if there was going to be water to fight fire?

The fire hall was right across the street from the church and on top of the fire hall was the siren. Many is the time when that siren sounded right in the middle of the service – of course the church emptied itself.

I can remember the struggle at home to keep warm. We had stoves and that was it. So we wore mittens and we wore plenty of rags. I can remember the driving winds that drove the cold in. Nowadays people are protected with better clothing. We got along some way and I think we even enjoyed it.

One little incident I remember as a pretty young kid – Dad and I were walking on the sidewalk between Douglas and the mine, and as we were walking along we would meet some of these Slavs, these people of foreign origin, and when they would see the minister coming they would get off the sidewalk and take off their hat and bow their heads as we walked by. And as a kid I thought boy, my Dad must be somebody. Oh that stuck with me. Ralph tells me that when Dad landed in Douglas he had a bolero hat and I know he also had a twisted up moustache, so he went uptown wearing that bolero hat and that twisted moustache and I guess he made quite an impression.

We stayed two years in Douglas. At the end of that time we were transferred over to Seward. That would be another thousand miles to the northwest.

Lisa: Joe, was there a church building already in Douglas when you arrived there?

Joe: Uh, yes, there was a church building in Douglas. Dad did not have to build it. It was a church – it was not something they hauled in – but it was small and probably quite inadequate, but it was there, provided by the mission board.

Lisa: What about a home? Was that provided?

Joe: I can't remember whether the home belonged to the church or whether we had to rent one. It must have been a home provided by the church, but it was a board house and it was not too well built, I know that.

Lisa: I just wondered because in Seward you had a different existence.

Joe: Very different. I want to mention how we got out of Douglas to go to Seward. Again we had to cross the Gastineau Channel and again by a small boat. Our steamboat would come to Juneau to pick us up, but we did not know when. So it was a case of get from Douglas over to Juneau, go to a hotel, live in a hotel until the boat came. And my recollection is that we lived almost two weeks in that hotel there. Who paid the bills I don't know.

SEWARD: 1905 – 1912

Joe: The steamer that took us from Juneau to Seward was the steamer *Portland*. She was a comparatively small vessel – steamboat – not very comfortable, not very nice to ride in, and during our trip we had a lot of very rough weather. The boat rocked and pitched and turned and twisted, and we even had a fire on board before we got to Seward, but we arrived in Seward I think it was November, on about Nov. 5. I was then five years old and we were taken to a hotel and stayed there for a few days until we could get the church tent put up.

The church tent was a tent about 20 by 30 feet and we had some kind of sleeping arrangement in the back of the church and a kind of drapery we would pull, and then church service was out in the front end of it. Our start in Seward was from scratch. We did not have a house to live in so Dad had to build a little shed which was to be our dormitory. There were four children – Fred and Ralph and I – three boys, slept in a double bunk bed and we had the upper layer.

Dad and Ruth and mother slept in the lower story down below us in that little shed-like dormitory.

Sometimes the wind would blow the snow in and we'd wake up in the morning and shake the snow off the covers – and it was always cold. Later on Dad put up a tent next to the dormitory building and that was our kitchen and dining room, and it was not too warm in there.

Dad had a way with the rough mining people and the prospecting type people. He seemed to know how to meet them, how to talk to them, and as soon as he had his church up he had the building full – people came. And I remember for a number of years the little congregation there flourished - went along in good style. Then we moved our living out of the church, out of the tent, and that gave us a larger tent for the church. Then as the years went by the tent church was boarded up until it became totally a board structure, and little by little it was made into a better type of thing.

Dad used to have his midweek services in there and of course he had the Sunday services, the Sunday school, we had our Christmas celebrations, and one thing I do remember particularly was those old rough people coming into the church and sitting down and oh how they sang! I've never heard singing that impressed me as that singing did. Those fellas, some of them pretty rough characters, seemed to enjoy it – they seemed to get a lot out of it.

Life in Seward I would say was better than Skagway but it was still pretty rough. Seward was a town that began as a railroad town. They were building what was then the Alaska Central Railway, now the government railway, and Seward was the saltwater terminus and they had their camp in Seward and they would take their workers out along the right of way to wherever the jobs were.

I do remember we had a lot of saloons because the men demanded it. A number of interesting things happened – one was the eruption of Mt. Katmai in 1912. Mt Katmai was about 200 miles away and she began to belch fire and smoke and finally the big eruption came and the whole top of the mountain was disintegrated – blew off – and the crater that was left afterward was a tremendous big hole. The largest diameter of that hole was three miles. Shorter diameters were less. The smoke and ash from that drifted our way and we had ash on the ground. We did not see the sun for over two weeks. And much of the vegetation was affected by the, I guess it was sulfur, in the ash.

Lisa: Could you see the eruption at all?

Joe: Oh yes I'm glad you asked that. We could. We saw the belching of the smoke and ash in to the air, but at night we even saw the flames 200 miles away. We would have seen much more had not the mountains, you know, kind of stopped our vision.

Lisa: Were you afraid?

Joe: Yes, we were all afraid. We had earthquakes all during that period of time. And we had as many as three and four a day, many of them were quite mild, once in a while we'd get a pretty good shaker and we were scared a bit – no doubt about that.

Dad built a manse if you want to call it that – they scooped out the hole in the ground for the basement and then they built the foundation out of logs. Not cement but logs. Seems to me the basement had a dirt floor. And on top of that log foundation he built a 1-1/2 story house, and the house was built quite well. That house stayed there and when I visited Seward in 1964 it was still there. Now it has since burned down. It's not there now. But that house went through the big earthquake of '64 and it was used as a place for the Red Cross to take care of people that were hurt. It was the one house in town that seemed to stand the earthquake very well.

Lisa: He must have really known how to build a house.

Joe: I might digress a little bit and say that Seward was a very beautiful situation. The mountains across the bay were an unending source of joy for us. We used to sit in our dining room window with the mountains across the bay and comment on the beauty there both in the winter and the summer. We always enjoyed that. Seward itself is a very beautiful town – very beautiful situation.

Are you interested in some family history?

Lisa: Sure.

Joe: Dad came from Norwegian parentage. His father and mother were living in Norway – the father was a carpenter and was working on a church steeple in Hammerfest, Norway, very far to the north. Mother, expecting my father to be born, was with her family in the central part of Norway. I think she had planned to remain there until the baby was born, but his father fell off that church steeple. As a result of that fall he died about two weeks later. But my grandmother then thought she should go to where he was and on that boat journey Dad was born on the high seas off the coast of Norway.

Dad and his mother moved to Chicago when he was about three years of age and then when he was maybe 6 or 7 or 8 they moved to Astoria, Ore., and made Astoria their home. Grandmother earned her living by knitting fishnets and Dad grew up in Astoria – that was his hometown there. He was there as a young man, sometimes fishing on the Columbia River, sometimes working in a grocery store, and when that situation was developing I think he then made up his mind or turned toward the ministry, and finally was taken into the church and became a young minister in Oregon.

I think that brings us up to where I started in.

Lisa: I wondered if you knew anything about how he got his further education after his formal schooling stopped?

Joe: Dad's education came through his self-efforts. I think while he was working as a grocery man he spent his evenings taking courses in the local YMCA and possibly some other night-school courses. Then later on he went to Portland, Oregon, for still further training, both day- and night-school training. Now maybe prior to that he was also in the Oregon State Militia, and it was his service in the militia that really brought him his citizenship, because moving to this country as the boy of three he wasn't sure whether he had citizenship. But at the end of his serving in the Oregon State Militia he was granted citizenship in the dismissal papers, so that was settled then.

Lisa: Was there a war going on then?

Joe: The militia was a little bit like the Coast Guard – more or less of a home guard. Any town of any size and any state had their militia in those days – they don't now – but they had uniforms and guns and everything.

Lisa: I just wondered because my Dad, being born in Sweden, got his citizenship through serving in World War I.

SKAGWAY: 1912 - 1918

Joe: Perhaps we could go along a little bit. After being in Seward for about eight years and bringing that little church from a tent church up to a pretty substantial church building, and leaving a good, strong program going there, then the bishop moved him to Skagway, Alaska.

The church there was pretty well established but it was under the Presbyterian Church. The Methodist Church also had a building there, and when the Methodists moved my Dad into Skagway the Presbyterian people really wanted that their church should be the one that would have the minister. They talked about it quite a bit. They talked to my Dad and asked if he would be willing to be under the Presbyterian Church. So it was arranged that he would change his affiliation. And he did so and became then a Presbyterian minister and still served at Skagway. And the Methodists literally returned the field to the Presbyterians. It was their field originally.

So the Presbyterians now have the old Methodist Church building and the old Presbyterian building – two properties – and they are conducting the work there. Dad stayed in Skagway about five years. We were there when the territory of Alaska voted to go dry. And we were there when some of the places went dry by local option. Dad was one of them who kind of prodded them along. But Skagway went dry by local option – then the territory went dry.

At that time, too, Mother was very active in the Women's Christian Temperance Union.

They stayed in Skagway – oh I remember that was in my teen years – and we were there until the family was pretty well grown up. I had reached the point where I decided to leave on my own. So I preceded the family from Skagway to Seattle and got myself a job, so as the family did come along, I think in the fall or some months later, they came out and Dad then became a YMCA chaplain in World War I. He was sent down to Fort Stevens at the mouth of the Columbia River – his old stomping ground. He was there quite a little while.

Lisa: How long was he a chaplain?

Joe: Oh it must have been a couple of years – until the end of the war – when the forts were abandoned and they began to fold up.

GAP IN TAPE.

LISA MUST HAVE STOPPED THE TAPE AND ASKED JOE TO GO BACK AND PROVIDE MORE DETAIL ABOUT THE SEWARD YEARS

Joe: The first winter – the winter of our arrival, and that would be the year 1905 – Dad put up a tent to serve as church and our living quarters. We lived in the very back part of that tent church. On Sundays they drew the drapery and conducted services in the front half or two-thirds of the church.

The next living quarters, which were accomplished before the oncoming winter, was to build a little dormitory shed in back of the church and to put an addition onto that which was a kitchen and that was a tent type of thing, with maybe low wooden walls.

So we lived in that structure then for probably about two winters. The first winter, 1905, was in the church tent, the next two winters, 1906 and 1907, in the dormitory kitchen combination. Now the (sic) third winter we moved across the street into a building and spent at least a part of the year in the building.

Lisa: Was that a house?

Joe: It was a house but not a residence. It was actually a little schoolhouse. While living there Dad began to build the manse or the residence. So that by the end of another year… (tape ends).

Appendix 3

Willard Seward Pedersen Interview
Oct. 5, 1911 – July 15, 2007

Interviewed by his nephew, Fred's, wife Lisa Pedersen

Transcribed by his nephew Dan Pedersen

Willard: Did Ruth say anything about Dad's mountain climbing activities?

Lisa: Well, a little bit, but she said the boys could…

Willard: Well all I know is hearsay because I was too small, but he was, I think, quite a hiker and outdoors person. The part I remember was when we were in Skagway. He used to do quite a bit of mountain climbing on mountains around there. There was a mountain in Skagway called A-B Mountain. I know he led very many parties up to the top of that.

Lisa: Wasn't there a club he formed for people who liked to go outdoors and climb and take pictures?

Willard: I don't know.

Ruth: There was an Alpine Club in Skagway, of which he was the moving spirit, and the teachers in the schools were active members. They set an age limit of 16, and it caused so much feeling between the young people and the parents that the four of us got together one day and wrote a poem, of which I have a copy here…we called them the Gay Alpiners.

Willard: There was an organization in Skagway called the Alaska Brotherhood. Was that any connection with this group?

Ruth: Yes, that was a fraternal organization originating in Skagway. The first chapter, Number 1, was in Skagway and they took A-B Mountain for their symbol because in the spring when the snow melted it always left the outline of these two letters plainly on the mountainside.

Willard: Yeah it did, A-B. I remember that. There is an Alaska Brotherhood Hall still in Skagway, and Joe is still a member of the Alaska Brotherhood, and he can show you his membership card if you ask him to. It's, uh, quite a unique building the way it is built, but getting back to Dad, other than the fact that I knew he was climbing and hiking in Alaska, my next memory of that sort of thing is Newhalem (Washington) in 1921, he did a lot of hiking up in there with Joe and with me, taking lots of photographs. This was at the time the City of Seattle was just constructing its power projects in that area. There was no dam at that time and no diversion tunnel for the water to come through, so they started constructing the Gorge Powerhouse as it is known today and boring a tunnel through the mountain where the water comes through today.

He used to do a lot of hiking in that area, which was very mountainous, and a lot of picture taking. Joe was with him on some of those trips and I was with him on a few. I'm not sure what Dad's status was. I think he was called a recreational director for the camp or for the construction contractor. He had a…I know that he preached services on Sunday in the recreational hall. On Friday nights we had a movie and he put that on. And there would be community singing groups of which he would preside, that sort of thing.

This was … Newhalem at that time was quite an isolated area – there was no road into that community. The only way to get in or out was on a little toonerville trolley from Rockport, and not many people did that in the wintertime. You couldn't, hardly, it was snowed in. Other than that I can't tell you much about his Newhalem activities – I think Joe should be able to tell you quite a bit.

Ruth: Here's a picture of the family sitting on the front porch in Newhalem.

Lisa: Oh. Well now, you only did, were in the 5th grade in Newhalem?

Willard: Yeah, I left. I went down – I might have been in the 6th grade also. The 5th and 6th grades I remember that now. For the 7th grade I went down and lived with Fred in Ilwaco, and for the 8th grade back up to Snohomish to live with Dad.

Lisa: Well at that time then Andy was living up there in Newhalem?

Willard: Yes he was. He was five years younger than I so he would have just been starting school.

Lisa: Did you go down to live with Fred because they didn't have a junior high?

Willard: I can't really tell you, Lisa, why. I don't remember. I think there are some aspects to that uh ... I didn't get along with my Stepmother very well. Neither did Andy. I think that was in the picture as one of the reasons I moved, although I'm not sure, though. This may have more true later, but I don't think so – I think I'm right. I think that's probably why I moved down with Fred.

Lisa: Now when you came back you lived with your Dad and Stepmother in Snohomish?

Willard: Yes, 8th grade through the first, second and third years of high school.

Lisa: So your senior year of high school you didn't?

Willard: Here in Seattle. I was back with Fred in Seattle. I don't know what else I can tell you about Dad – I wish I knew more. There are thousands of pictures and I've got some of them. Dad was a hobbyist, I think, very much so. He liked to take pictures. In later years he did some printing – used to print the church bulletins. In his earlier years he used to mimeograph the bulletins. In connection with the pictures he took he would make lanternslides, as they called them in those days. They were 4- by 5-inch glass plated slides and he even colored them with oil, and he would put on illustrated lectures at church services. They would show slides and sing songs – it was a forerunner of today's home movies and slide shows.

Lisa: Was that while you were in Alaska or here…?

Willard: He used to do it up there. He also did it in Newhalem. I know he did it in Alaska because I have at home now perhaps three dozen of those glass slides he worked on, but we don't have any projector to show them on.

Lisa: Those projectors probably are hard to come by…

Willard: Oh I think they would be. You can get them professionally I think.

Lisa: Would those be travel slides or slides in connection with sermons maybe?

Willard: Well, both. He would do a series of slides, for example, that would be shown while you're singing a church hymn. And as the hymn was being sung he would project one slide for a few seconds and then another slide would come on. I can't remember the hymns, but they would just be beautiful scenes that would come onto the screen during the singing of the song.

Ruth: They went east to New York before your day, of course, when he was raising money for the YMCA in Seward.

Willard: I understand he did. And I know I've heard him give lectures on Alaska after they came back here in which he would use those same slides over again, and this would be more travelogue type.

Lisa: What do you remember of your Mother. Do you remember anything?

Willard: Really very little. I remember what she looked like, but her personality I don't remember much about.

Lisa: What can you tell me about your Dad's personality, if you had to capsulize it. Besides being a photographer and an outdoor enthusiast, did he have a personality similar to Fred or was he entirely different?

Willard: I don't know. He had interest in a lot of things. He was a good carpenter. A good photographer. He was a good printer when he was printing his own church bulletins. I think he was a gregarious person. Did Ruth mention the fact he taught school for a while when we were in Auburn?

Lisa: We hadn't gotten that far.

Willard: One of the things that kind of impressed me was that here was a man who went up to Alaska in the very early days, I don't know what Dad's formal education was but I don't think it was much, but he accumulated somewhere along the line a vast collection of books – good books. He had a big library in Seward and Skagway and Newhalem and Snohomish and Bellingham. He had books on literature and religion – I was always amazed. I don't know how he ever accumulated, how he had the money to do it. But he did have a lot of books and my memory is that in Auburn he did teach in the high school for a time. Is that not right Ruth?

Ruth: I had forgotten that, Willard, but I think you're right.

Willard: I'm sure he did, for quite some period of time. By that I mean most of a school year as a temporary teacher for some reason. The reason why I don't know.

Ruth: He taught in Skagway.

Willard: He did?

Ruth: Yes.

Lisa: What did he teach in Auburn?

Willard: I think it was either history or English.

Lisa: What year do you think that was?

Willard: It would have been 1920. 1920 I think. Because he left there in 21. I think he probably came in 1919.

Ruth: I think that's right. He came in 1918 and lived on Vashon Island for a while.

Willard: And then we lived here in Seattle, in Rainier Valley for a time, too. I remember they were living there when the World War I armistice was signed.

Ruth: Yes!

I can't find that poem *(about the Alpiners). At this point Ruth begins to recite the poem from memory:*

> **The Alpiners are a bunch of gays**
>
> **It's great to see them at their play**
>
> **To leave the youngsters by the road**
>
> **Is now considered a la mode.**

Willard: Dad went to Skagway as a Methodist minister. My understanding always was that among the various Protestant denominations that were active in Alaska, namely the Methodist Church, Presbyterian Church, perhaps the Episcopal and maybe the Catholic, although I'm not sure they were part of it, there was an understanding among these churches that they would not compete with each other. In Skagway there wasn't any active Presbyterian Church. I'm not sure about that but I don't think so.

Ruth: There was a comity agreement between the two denominations.

Willard: So Dad went there as a Methodist and he was a Methodist in Seward as well. And he was in Skagway for, what, three years or perhaps four, and the story I always heard was that the time came when the Methodists would leave and the Presbyterians would come in. Dad liked the area and wanted to stay, and became a Presbyterian instead of a Methodist so he could stay. And from then on he was a Presbyterian minister.

Willard: There was another aspect to it I think – the feeling was that the Presbyterian Church had a little better pension system than the

Methodists. (Fades out). Anyway he did make the switch and stayed at the same church with the same congregation.

Ruth: As I recall he stayed under the Presbyterian Church for the first year on a temporary basis with the understanding that he did not lose his Methodist relationship. At the end of that year he liked the Presbyterian form of government so much that he decided he would like to remain Presbyterian.

Willard: The Pedersen family left Skagway in the fall of 1918 and the original plan, as I understand it is that they were going to go south on the Princess Sophia. They had the tickets ready to go for a particular date, and for some reason it was necessary for us to change the departure date, so we came out one trip before that on the Princess Sophia.

And on the next trip when she came south from Skagway, she had an accident, running into some rocks called Vanderbilt Reef in Lynn Canal between Skagway and Juneau. I think there were over 300 people on board. She was sitting high on the reef, apparently safe, and there were some smaller ships that came close by offering to take some of the passengers off. The story was that the captain wouldn't let the passengers go because he thought it wasn't safe for them to do so. There was another aspect, which was that another of the Canadian line vessels was to arrive the next day to take the passengers off.

So anyway the skipper decided not to let anyone off, and in the night a heavier storm came up and the ship shifted off the reef and sank, and everyone was lost.

This maritime accident resulted in a very famous lawsuit in the federal courts that eventually went to the U.S. Supreme Court on the question of the limitation of liability of the ship owner for the damages resulting from the loss of life and loss of property as a result of the accident. The decision as I remember reading it, was that the ship line was able to limit its liability to the value of the ship as it lay sunk in the water of Lynn Canal, which was nothing of course. Anyway, I've always felt we were fortunate to come down one trip sooner than we did.

Ruth: Willard, it was my understanding that the reason for putting our departure up one trip was that a large party of miners were coming out from Canada, having completed their summer's work, and had asked to take over the ship for that particular trip, and the local authorities asked our folks if they would mind moving up one trip.

Willard: Was it the skipper or purser on the ship who was a close friend of Dad's?

Ruth: The stewardess was a close friend, a very close friend, and I don't recall the other officers. But the stewardess always came to church when she was in port.

Willard: Lisa, did Ruth tell you about the glacier? There is a glacier on the Seward Peninsula called Pedersen Glacier, that's named after Dad. How it got to be named after Dad, all I know is hearsay. The story I heard was that the U.S. Coast and Geodetic Survey was surveying the area, and the officer who was in charge of that unit was a friend of Dad's. There are a lot of glaciers in that area and they had to name them after somebody, and he got chosen for one of them.

Lisa: So that isn't in Glacier Bay?

Willard: No, this is touch of Seward on the Kenai Peninsula.

Ruth: Incidentally, the name of that man who named the glacier for Dad, his name was Brooks, and he is the man for whom the Brooks Range is named.

(BREAK IN THE TAPE)

Ruth: I'm coming in after Willard has been talking and one of his remarks was to the effect that he thought he had inherited many of our Father's characteristics. Since his statement I've been sitting here mentally reviewing the attributes of my father and comparing him with Willard, and I find many similarities, with some rather marked differences also.

Willard is skilled in many arts. He does technically perfect photographic work. He makes his own picture frames, which are made without a flaw, finished professionally with many layers of varnish and the proper rubbing with sandpaper to get them polished, the corners mitered just so, and he takes a great deal of pride in turning out a beautiful end result.

He does cabinetwork. He knows how to maintain a beautiful lawn around his house. He knows the technique of spraying the trees. He's learned how to run a sailboat since his son has developed that interest – all this on top of being a successful corporation attorney. I find Willard is quite pensive; a little quiet in a group, very seldom exposes his inner feelings. I recall that as a child Willard was greatly affected by music. In fact he was quite an annoyance to me because very often in the evening I would sit down at the piano after he had gone to bed and I would be playing ... soulfully! And presently Willard would come running into the living room with tears streaming down his face. Nothing was the matter with him except Ruth was playing and he couldn't stand it.

Lisa: Does he have musical ability?

Ruth: He's very sensitive to music. As a young man he sang. He has a nice voice. He sang in choral groups and now with his wife he has interest in opera and high-class music with a high standard for the production.

My Father also enjoyed music. I think I mentioned the records he maintained. I think my Father was perhaps a little more outgoing, a little more gregarious than Willard is – a ready handshake, a ready smile, and a quick realization of the needs of the other person.

In some of these pamphlets which Willard brought today reference is made by one of the writers to L.H. Pedersen, who was sent to Douglas, as being a very satisfactory minister in that he was able to renovate the worn out, rundown church and parsonage and make it more livable. They had found some satisfaction in his services there, including that item. Therefore, they felt safe in appointing him, with his wife and four children, to go to Seward, where the Methodists owned a piece of land with no provision for sleeping quarters, eating quarters, or otherwise making it livable for some time, as we've talked about in the past.

I think my Father liked a challenge. And his best work was where he met people stripped of their superficialities, bedrock, down to the quick of life. I mentioned once happily that he liked to sing and had a fair voice. I think if he'd had some training he would have been quite good, but singers were scarce and far between, so following the moment of that day I've heard him sing at a church service, "Where's My Wandering Boy Tonight?" He would emote appropriately, and the women in the church sanctuary would wipe their eyes appropriately, and I think it relieved tensions and created a feeling of oneness between this wandering boy and others that they didn't tell about.

I think some of the same differences existed between my father and my brother, Fred, too.

Fred had a little different approach to people than my father. Fred's best work was as an executive…

Transcriber's note: For the continuation of this thought, see the Ruth Pedersen interview.

Appendix 4

Ruth Pedersen Haugen Interview
1902 –1987

Interviewed in April 1978 by her nephew Fred's wife, Lisa Pedersen
Transcribed November 2000 by her nephew, Dan Pedersen

My Dad and Mother were appointed to the Methodist work in Douglas, Alaska, in about 1903 from the old Columbia River Conference of the Methodist Church. Since I was only a few months old when they journeyed forth to that country I don't remember Douglas, but in 1905 they were transferred to the Methodist work in Seward, Alaska, and from there on my memory got pretty high.

You might be interested to know that my parents originally had pledged themselves to do missionary work in India. At the time of their marriage they had made a vow to go into fulltime missionary work as soon as they could prepare for it. Particularly, my Father wanted more education and he wanted to develop his own resources and become an accredited minister in the Methodist Church.

So after this had been accomplished, as you will notice in some of the clippings I have given you today, he and my Mother went to Conference in accord with the Methodist Church form of government, expecting that year to be appointed to India as fulltime foreign missionaries. And their names were read and appointed to India. At that time there were three boys in the family.

Soon after Conference it became apparent that Ruth was on the way. So when the Bishop learned that another child was imminent the appointment was delayed for a year until conference time the following year. And my parents again went to Conference full of anticipation because they were going to at last fulfill their vows taken at the time of marriage and be on their way to India. So imagine their consternation at the time of reading of the appointments at Conference to find that instead of being sent to India they were to be sent to Alaska.

Horrors! What a place to go. India was all right. You could get used to lions and snakes, dirty people and dirty air, but Alaska! That place of snow and ice, Eskimos and wild Indians. Heaven forbid the Lord surely didn't call them to go there.

So they went home and prayed about it and finally decided that some way or other they would be given the strength and courage to fulfill their appointment. *I can recall my mother saying more than once that she would think ahead to the Alaska days and all she could see was four little mounds of snow with four little white crosses above them.* But in later years she would brag that they had brought out six children with them, all alive and well.

My brother Joe has some memories of Douglas, some of which I think are quite…what do I want to say, quite meaningful to the family. I've heard Joe tell how in Douglas, which was a mining town, and the town was full of, as I recall, Slovaks who worked in the mines, they had a great respect for the clergyman. Joe, who was 2-1/2 years my senior, would tell how he walked down the street hand in hand with his Papa as he was called in those days and the feeling of pride and feeling of being a very special tall young boy because as they would walk along the street some of those Slovak men would step of the street, take off their hat and bow to my father, as was the tradition.

I've heard Fred tell in relation to Douglas how the older boys, again about 10 and 12 I would think, maybe a little older, they were grilled by my parents in what to do in case of fire. Douglas was in the middle of the Williwaw wind country. The temperatures would drop down below zero and one of these winds would blow. The houses were not very strong, not very secure, and a fire once it got started would quickly sweep across a building or a block or a town. My Father and the two older boys never went to bed at night without laying out their protective clothing – warm hat and coat and boots and gloves – so that in case of fire they could get out in a moment and help not only our own selves but neighbors if it was needed.

Lisa: What did they have to put out a fire then?

Ruth: I suppose water and fire hoses. We did in Seward, but I just can't imagine anything else. In 1905 my folks were transferred to Seward from Douglas. The LaViolette family occupied the Methodist parsonage in Seward *(Transcriber's note: She must have meant Juneau)* and I've heard my parents relate how, while waiting for transportation to Seward by steamship, they stayed with the LaViolette family in Juneau.

They were two families in one small little parsonage with several children apiece and I guess the quarters were pretty cramped. And their oldest offspring and my oldest brother had a falling out which lasted all through the years until they were married in 1916 – that was Ethel Josephine LaViolette.

For 10 days they waited in the LaViolette home for the whistle of the steamer Portland coming in to dock in Juneau, and I guess they were some pretty tense 10 days, and I think it was during that time my father shaved his moustache off.

Then finally the steamship Portland arrived and the Pedersen family boarded. I don't have many memories of that trip except one. My father had made me a little red wagon - this was another one of his skills, carpentry work, which he inherited probably from his father who was a skilled craftsman in wood. He'd made me a little red wagon with a long tongue on it and two little wooden wheels, which I could pull around beside me. And I vividly recall my brother Joe and me standing at the rear of the boat, looking out over the stern and watching the path left in the water by the propeller of the boat. And I had the little red wagon and Joe looked at me and said, *"Throw it overboard and see what it does."* I said *"Uh uh."* He says, *"Come on, it'll be fun."* So over it went, and at the moment of parting I knew I'd never see it again – it was a horrible memory.

But I guess my folks made me realize that I didn't always have to obey what my brothers told me.

Lisa: What kind of boat was it, do you remember?

Ruth: It was a small steamship. The "Portland" was very historic and carried many of the people going to the gold rush in '98 – it had quite a long history – not a large boat as boats go, I probably should say ship, but anyway it was seaworthy and crossing the Gulf of Alaska was, as usual, quite stormy. I know that my folks were seasick and one morning as we neared the entrance to Seward harbor my father hadn't been able to sleep. He'd gotten up and was walking the deck at 5 in the morning, only to learn that his sleep had been disturbed by the efforts of the crew to put out a fire in the hold, which had come close to being quite serious, but which was under control by the time we reached Seward.

Arriving in Seward, my father left us aboard ship while he went uptown to find a place to pitch a tent for us to sleep in that night.

Lisa: A tent?

Ruth: A tent. He had a large A-frame tent that had been provided most graciously by the Methodist Church and this was to be our place of residence for two winters. Uh, he got the tent up and got some of the furnishings into the tent so that we all had a place to sleep that night – I think some of the townspeople saw to it that we had food for a couple of days – but that tent is full of memories.

Eventually Dad put a board floor in the tent and boarded up the sides so as to shut out the cold as much as possible and then put a tarpaulin over the roof separated by a long ridgepole so there was space between the roof of the tent and the tarpaulin, which made for some airspace, which I understand helped to keep us a little warmer. Inside there was a little airtight heater and probably a four-hole kitchen stove with a little oven in it and we soon learned that the oven was a great place to heat a rock.

Each one of us had our own special rocks to keep warm with, and as we sat around eating our meals there would be a hot rock under our feet, and at night those rocks went to bed with us, nicely wrapped in old blankets or old sheets, something of that kind. You could cuddle up to them pretty well—not bad.

Lisa: A hot rock?

Ruth: A hot rock. Much better than a hot water bottle because they didn't freeze.

Lisa: What did you have on the floor before he put the wooden flooring in?

Ruth: To tell the truth I don't remember unless it was canvas.

Lisa: What about the furnishings?

Ruth: Well, there were two or three straight chairs. There were kitchen utensils. He built two bunks for sleeping purposes but of course there would have to be bedding. The bunks were kind of interesting because Fred and Ralph and Joe slept in the upper bank, and Dad and Mother and myself were in the lower bunk. First thing every morning that Dad would do would be to pick up the four corners of the tarp that covered the lower bunk and shake the snow out onto the floor. Then he would take up the broom that was by the side of the bed and sweep the snow outside that had accumulated during the night, and then start the fire.

Lisa: Well now where did the snow come in from?

Ruth: Cracks and I think it just was osmosis. It came from somewhere.

But we lived through that for two winters and as I look back on it I thought it was quite a lark, you know, for a youngster who didn't know anything else in those days. And finally – before too long – he built a shanty leaning up against the tent and the next thing was to pitch a tent for the church. That was the place where he held meetings and with his own hands he made benches for people to sit on.

The benches had no backs. You just sat on rough wooden benches and in time he got backs on them too, but much of this was done with his own skill at carpenter work. He was able to meet the people of the community, which was about 200 people as I recall at the time, on a one-to-one basis. Of course in Alaska nobody has a past. I'm not suggesting that we carried one, but you never asked questions of anybody.

The church activity soon became the social center of the town. There soon was a Ladies Aid organized which was a great asset to the work of the church. I should make it plain right here that while they were termed missionaries they were not missionaries to the Indians, particularly, but more to the white people, because Seward actually didn't have very many Indians at that time. There were a few Indians, a few Eskimos.

Lisa: Was there any other church in Seward?

Ruth: Yes, the Episcopal Church had gone in ahead of us and there was a very fine relationship between the Episcopal Church and the Methodist Church. Also the Catholic Church was there and again there was a very warm feeling among the three little congregations.

Lisa: Now did they have tents or did they have buildings by the time you came?

Ruth: The Episcopal Church had a very nice building. I don't know whether it was built by the Russian occupation – I don't think so. The Episcopal Church (was) under the direction of Bishop Rowe, who was historically well known in Alaska. Whether he had caused it to be built (I don't know), but it was a church of such structure and beauty that it's still famous for its architecture and paintings inside, and I recall that in 1965 when my brothers Fred and Joe and I traveled to Seward for the 60th anniversary of the founding of the church, Joe reminded me that he had started his schoolwork in the basement of the Episcopal Church there in Seward, which I had forgotten, but we visited it and it was still standing as I remembered it.

Where are we?

Lisa: I got you off track because I asked you if the other churches had tents.

Ruth: It might be interesting to comment on the warm feeling that existed between the churches. The Methodist Church was more or less the social center of the town. The Ladies Aid society would have ice cream socials, they would have Japanese tea, it was really quite a social center, and they managed to have enough of these events that they raised a little money and bought a bell that was mounted on a high delicate (?) post for the church and it was quite historic because it became the fire alarm for the town, too. And they purchased an organ for the church, a little foot-pumped organ,

Lisa: Now was this in the tent?

Ruth: By this time the tent had been boarded over and made into a more weatherproof building. Dad used to say not every church provided free sleeping quarters for the incapacitated members of the church or those who came from the back hills, from the mining country, to the church for session. It was very convenient to slip into one of the bunks back behind the church and sleep it off…

And we youngsters were taught not to disturb the members. I'm afraid I'm rambling but these memories come as you're talking and you get them out of order probably. Going back to the interplay of the churches and the camaraderie that existed, the public Christmas tree was always held in the Methodist Church complete with gifts that were brought to the church and placed on the tree where the gift exchange took place. And Santa Claus came in the north window with a dog team and sleigh bells. And always when the Catholic Church had their Christmas exercise the Methodist minister's children were invited and there was always a gift on the tree for each of the Methodist youngsters, which we thought was a very nice touch, especially if it had popcorn in it.

You might also be interested in the fact that after my folks had been there for a while and began their ministry, they found a great need among the natives and half-breeds who lived on the beaches at Seward in rather disheveled condition.

And one family by the name of Lowell, which that's an interesting sidelight too, was found to be in extremely poor circumstances. The children were dirty, infested with vermin, and the mother was sick in bed, dying of tuberculosis. The father was a half-breed related to the poet James Russell Lowell. His father was the brother of James Russell Lowell.

This brother had taken a common-law wife and this family was the offspring. And the folks tried to help them with clothing and food and fuel, and one day the folks went down and found a tiny baby nursing a dead mother. A little black-eyed, black-haired boy, two weeks old. So the father, who was known locally as Billy Lowell, was of course grief stricken – he didn't know what to do with the baby. He picked it up, put it in my mother's arms, *"Mrs. Pedersen, he yours. You take. He yours. This my Johnny – he yours."* So my folks took the baby home and plans were made for them to adopt him legally. We all loved him, little Johnny, big black eyes, dark hair, but he didn't have a chance. And as I recall he lived approximately a year when he died.

Well his folks were from the Russian Catholic branch of the church and the Lowell family still wanted the Russian Catholic priest, so I can recall the Catholic priest coming into Seward and conducting a service not from the pulpit but from the entrance way to the church because their faith would not allow them to occupy a Protestant pulpit at that time. But I remember the little coffin where the baby lay, the little child lay, and the two fully robed Russian priests shaking the incense. from their …… and I couldn't understand what they were doing to Johnny, it bothered me… But we loved Johnny very much.

LOUIS AND FANNY

Let's see. Seward was a small community. At that time the Alaska Central Railway was running out of Seward and that's really what kept the town alive.

And some of the prominent people, the Aladdins (?) for one, the Hales, who were the bankers, and some other people who helped to operate the town, the Barretts (?) of the powerhouse, developed a little aristocracy in a way to which my folks were soon made a part.

One of the events of the town would be the arrival of the boat from Seattle, which came about once a month. Seward was the terminus of that end of the run and on arrival in Seward they would usually remain over one full night, possibly two, waiting for people there to pick up their mail, read it, answer it and get it back on the same boat. Of course freight came in and had to be unloaded for town supplies, and everything stopped and went into action for the arrival of the boat, and if there were tourists aboard as happened in the summertime – tourists – there would usually be a dance hastily put together which was over the old Brown & Hawkins store. There was a dance hall there, and my parents always went.

Lisa: What was Brown & Hawkins?

Ruth: That was a big mercantile store. Groceries, miner's supplies, haberdashery of a sort, that sort of thing.

I think there would be somebody at the piano as I recall. A few times I was permitted to go by my parents to this dance, knowing that it was not the thing for good Methodists to do, but still realizing that it was an event of the town in which _____ socially and it couldn't be all bad, and so my folks would go down and stay through the first dance. And having made their appearance and being recognized, made to feel really a part of the social life of the town, they would depart.

Lisa: Did they dance?

Ruth: No.

Lisa: No?

Ruth: No they didn't. Those Methodist people didn't dance.

Lisa: Shucks.

Ruth: Right. So I would sit there and look at those beautiful people dancing and it just looked like so much fun, but I knew: No, Ruth didn't do that!

So I think I was telling you before we started recording that my father had many interests besides Missionary work. He was a very skilled photographer: in fact he supplemented his missionary income by making postcards in wholesale quantities. And always with the arrival of the boat in Seward during the tourist season, tourists would come to the house while the folks got out the large sample albums with postcards – it would be scenes of the mountains in their grandeur, mountains and water, scenes of ships, maybe the ship on which they'd just arrived, and often many of the tourists would be reporters for newspapers or magazines, such as that.

And they would usually come up to the parsonage which my father had built--by this time we were in a nice home – and give their orders for so many hundred of these cards. Which meant that on their departure my father and my two older brothers would go down to the basement where he had full photographic equipment and spend that night getting out this order so as to have it to give to the tourist people the next day.

And I have visions of these postcards drying on these racks which my father had made – large racks on which these postcards had been laid out to dry overnight – and the next morning he'd take a straight edge and straighten out the photographs or postcards I should say, and recheck the count and make sure every print was a good copy, not too dark, not too light, and get them to the hands of the person who had ordered them.

LOUIS AND FANNY

As a matter of fact the night the parsonage burned, when Willard was a tiny baby, some of the tourists had been dinner guests in our home that evening. My Mother had gotten out her damask table cloth, a few choice pieces of cut glass on which she was proud to serve, and there'd been a dinner. After that they remained to look over these sample albums of postcards they could order, and my Mother started up the stairs to put Willard to bed, who was then about three months old. Coming back into the living room where these guests were seated, busy around the table with the albums, my Mother said in a very weak little voice, *"Louie, I think our house is on fire."*

Lisa: My gosh.

Ruth: So with that my Dad and my older brothers jumped to get the fire extinguisher out of the kitchen, where it was always ready. Fred grabbed the fire extinguisher to go up the stairs to see if he could extinguish it, and realizing that the fire was beyond that treatment he turned around to come down the stairs with the extinguisher still squirting.

And out the front door went one of the tourists with Willard in her arms. It was the middle of January, the front steps were covered in ice, and she recalled afterwards how she had told my Mother that she would take the baby and go to the nearest house. And Mother looked at her and at the fine clothes she was wearing, because she was going to a dance afterwards, clothes including high-heeled pumps. And Mother, thinking of the ice on the steps and this woman who didn't understand our weather and our kind of footing, said, *"All right but don't kill him."*

And as the woman was just going down the front steps she was hit by the discharge of the fire extinguisher she slipped and went down four steps, five steps, clutching the baby in her arms, and she said afterwards, *"I was afraid to look – that is when I knew what she had meant."* But nothing came of it; neither she nor the baby was hurt.

But the days of the arrival of the tourists and the ordering of photographs were real events and the whole family gathered around to help out.

And incidentally, that was probably the way that Father was able to help the two older boys through the university. His photographs were circulated all over Alaska. The one of two bears fighting was probably his most famous one – those two little bears were my pet bears.

Lisa: Say Ruth, just to back up a little bit, how did they ever get the fire out if they couldn't do it with the extinguisher?

Ruth: Well, there was a volunteer fire department. And I mentioned this bell a while ago. My mother said to me, go over and ring the fire bell—it was about half a block from the parsonage at that time. Well, I had been so trained never to go outside without being fully clothed, that with the house burning over my head I put on my overshoes, my leggings, my coat, my fur cap and my mittens.

Laughter.

I was well trained, and then dashed out through four feet of snow to go over to the church to ring the fire bell. One side of the rope you would pull for church, the other side was for the fire bell – that made a dingdong, dingdong, dingdong – you knew that was fire. So presently there came a hand-pulled fire hose cart and I don't remember what other pieces of equipment were there, but the volunteer fire department was soon there, and as I stood pulling on that bell one of the firemen came over to me and said, *"Ruth, you can quit pulling that rope now, the firemen are here."*

But I said, *"Our house is burning and it's still burning, you haven't got it out, I'm going to keep on ringing,"* and I did. I think by this time Joe was helping me.

Laughter.

The fire gutted the attic and the upstairs and just on the downstairs the loss was by smoke and water, as well as the fire. Dad was mainly concerned about the photographic equipment, which was down in the basement. He had built this parsonage with double walls, so there was an air space between the two walls, and the smoke from the fire had gone down between the walls into the basement and none of us had gone to the basement for any reason for several hours. If anyone had gone down into the basement they would have known something was wrong. But it was quite a night.

Lisa: Do you remember how long it took them to put it out? Was it a long time?

Ruth: Oh, I'd say a couple of hours. I remember that the hotel in town gave us rooms. I don't recall who fed us. Everybody lost their clothes except me. I had a room downstairs and my clothes were under the stairway. They were damaged ...

Lisa: Was that in the dead of winter?

Ruth: January.

The fire they felt was caused by a crack in the flue caused by earthquakes – we had many earthquakes there. They were little jolts, they were just part of everyday life.

Another thing that happened would be snow slides. Up the canyon there was a large glacial stream that came down in back of our house and the canyon from which this stream emanated was the source of water intake for the power plant. There was always a man stationed up there at the intake to _____ so we had drinking water – piped water – to our homes. But it was also at the foot of a long draw. In the spring or if it was too warm a day there was the danger of snow slides.

We all knew the sound of that distant thunder – we'd say, *"A snow slide!"* Everybody would freeze for a moment and then would come the anxiety, "I wonder if whoever was on duty at the intake was caught in the snow slide." All the men in town would rush up there – my memory probably is not too accurate on this, but I'd guess a mile or two miles up the canyon – to go and look out for the man's safety. I recall that some were buried in the snow and were dug out and were ok, and others lost their lives. But that awful noise in the background is a noise you never forget.

Lisa: How many would you have in a year?

Ruth: Oh, two or three. Maybe not every year, either. But enough that we knew what that sound was. And then this glacier stream would get to overflowing every so often and would flood, and they'd have to put up bulkheads and rocks and sandbags, barriers to keep the water out, and sometimes the water would seep through and come down through the town. Town was on a slight slope heading down to the bay…

Lisa: When would that be?

Ruth: In the spring. The men would be out working and I recall the women going out with hot coffee and sandwiches to feed the men while they dammed up the glacier stream. It was another of the events that brought people together. Everyone was on a common level whether you were a stevedore or banker or whatever.

Lisa: Can we back up to the tent part before your father built the house? How long were you in the tent?

Ruth: We were in the tent two winters. Then we moved into a three-room house, which consisted of a living room, bedroom, kitchen.

Lisa: I recall your mentioning in the past having a separate tent for cooking and a separate tent for sleeping.

Ruth: That was when the shanty was built – the bunks were in the shanty and the tent became the kitchen

Lisa: Oh I see. So the tent remained as a kitchen and the shanty was the sleeping area?

Ruth: The heater was in the shanty. I recall the kitchen being closed up – rather tightly – after every meal.

LOUIS AND FANNY

Lisa: That was heated just by the cooking? What did you use for fuel?

Ruth: Wood. Yes, you see that was almost virgin country at that time and the two older brothers would go out and chop the wood or sometimes they would buy it from teamsters and stack it in the back yard. I used to know what a cord was because of the way it was stacked, and the men for their exercise would go out and saw up the wood for the wood stove, and in later years we began to burn coal, which would hold a fire.

Lisa: All the time in the tent you were wood-heated?

Ruth: Yes and our water supply was obtained by melting snow and ice. And on Saturday night, the snow and ice was removed from the yard and put into he washer boiler and heated, and I recall particularly after we moved into this little three-room house the kitchen was a little larger and they put the round wash tub in front of the oven which would be _____ on Saturday night. Ruth was still a baby at that time so she would get the first bath and I think my mother would get the second bath in the same water, and then the third person must be Joe, and then that water would be thrown out, and then a fresh supply of water would be put in and the three remaining people would get their baths then.

Lisa: They did that in order of seniority then?

Ruth: More or less...my Dad would be the last one. He was very meticulous and took care of himself adequately.

Uh, after this baby died, there were four older children, which the father, Billy Lowell, wanted my folks to also adopt. That was just a little bit more than they could manage so Mother took them over to the Baptist orphanage on _____ island near Kodiak, she was able through the church to get these four children into that home, and I recall they were in our home for oh several weeks while awaiting transportation over to this Baptist orphanage.

Lisa: How old were they?

Ruth: I would say probably from four up to 12 or 13, and I recall being sent out of the house one day while some of the members of the Ladies Aid were deeply engrossed with these children – there was something going on and I was dying to know what – so as I peeked through the window from the outside looking in, they were going after these children's hair with little fine-toothed combs and coal oil...

Lisa: What were they doing, removing lice?

Ruth: Yes.

Lisa: Oh! (Laughter)

Ruth: They didn't want the lice to propagate any further. I looked through the window and couldn't quite figure out what they were doing – I thought they were picking their brains out.

Lisa: Who told you?

Ruth: Oh, I think my Mother. She had quite a sense of humor.

There was quite an aristocracy in the town – there would be card parties, which proper Methodists did not attend, but other people, and when their children had birthdays, there would always be a birthday party in which I was always included, and then as the youngest member of the minister's family and the only little girl I knew I received many special favors which I wouldn't have otherwise, which I got from the miners.

These men would come to town and during the summer months they would hike out to the outlying mines for weeks at a time, trying to prove their claim. They had to do something during the summer months to help pass the time. I remember especially one miner brought me oh the most enchanted little house I've ever laid eyes on. He had used a platform, which I would guess was three or four feet long and two feet wide, on which he had built a perfect little log house. The log house was made of the limbs of little willow trees. The corners had interstices, there were windows in the proper places, the roof was sloping, covered over with sand which had been glued on, and out in front of the house was a little a place where you put a piece of wood to saw it. The saw was a buck saw, but this rack on which you put the wood was made by hand, and every house had one.

And there was a chair made of tiny little willow branches, a little rocking chair out in front. It was really a treasure.

Lisa: Whatever happened to the house?

Ruth: I guess we left it in Seward when we moved from Seward.

And another one gave me a watch. I had many gifts – music goodies, the miners would bake them sometimes. But it was amazing, realizing that they even thought about you and wanted to do something. I realize many times they wanted to say thank you for the homemade bread my mother sent to them. It wouldn't be proper to give a gift to the minister's wife so the youngster got it. I was the only daughter.

Lisa: It was always the daughter, not the boys?

Ruth: I was young and irresistible.

Lisa: Was that when you had the little pet bears?

Ruth: Yes, those bears were one of the gifts they brought to me.

Lisa: How long did you have the bears?

Ruth: I don't remember – several weeks. They were chained to large stones or blocks over in the yard of the jail. They were on locked chains so they wouldn't wander around. We would go over every day with food from our house and play with them, and later I was criticized for it because the hunter said they were very dangerous. I have one picture of a bear, which I can show you, of a bear on my back. I thought, *"Oh, this is a nice little affectionate bear,"* but the hunter said that was dangerous because with one slap of its paw it could take out an eye.

We finally sent them off to Woodland Park in Seattle.

Lisa: Now is that the bear that broke the window? I never did get that straight.

Ruth: No, she was loose, she lived in the hills out behind the town, and would forage in the community every so often. I told you she was named Carrie Nation, and she would come down and seemed to like the smell of the bars, the saloons, and if there was no way of getting in she would take care of that – she'd wham the window with her paw. I guess they finally caught her. She could really – she was a little dangerous at the time, those windows were hard to replace in those days.

Lisa: Oh, she did this on several occasions?

Ruth: Yes, she was looking for food.

Lisa: Would she go into the tavern then?

Ruth: I don't think she could get in.

Lisa: There was one that was sent to Woodland Park, right?

Ruth: Oh, there were many at different times.

Lisa: I remember Fred saying he went to Woodland Park to see a bear from Seward.

Ruth: I wouldn't be surprised.

Lisa: I thought it was Carrie Nation but maybe it wasn't.

Ruth: I don't think it was Carrie Nation – she wouldn't have been alive that long.

Well let's see, where are we?

LOUIS AND FANNY

Dad would go off on a trek every summer, on a hiking expedition, into the backwoods country and to the mines, and taking with him usually one of the boys. Father and son would get to know each other in a way at that time that they wouldn't otherwise. Dad learned a great deal of woods lore, he learned the rules of hiking and mountaineering, he led a troop of Boy Scouts to whom he taught the same. But on these hikes into the hill country they'd usually be gone about two weeks with a backpack on their backs, hunting up these lonely men who were out in the hills all by themselves, and for whom the sight of a fellow human being was a ray of sunshine. And I think father and son got very close to each other during that time.

And he also got very close to these lonely men. They looked forward to his coming; they had a great understanding of each other. I always felt that my father's greatest work as a minister was when he carried the gospel to these people. His attributes were along the interests of pioneering, rather than the formal, organized church – he liked the informality of the pioneer atmosphere, the openness. He felt that he was one of them.

There was a loyalty that developed that was really quite unique. During the long winter months the miners would often walk back to town and we got to know the many characters. There was One Eyed Charlie, there was Old Man Bill, there was Johnny the Janitor, and incidentally my father was known as Parson Pete.

These people relished coming to the parsonage, maybe having a home-cooked meal, maybe being part of family life for an evening, and feeling that they weren't altogether outcasts, because many of the men came up to Alaska as a last resort to either end it all or forget the past.

Lisa: Now did any of them strike it rich?

Ruth: It depends on what you call rich. I have no memory of any of them getting rich, unfortunately.

END OF TAPE

DAN PEDERSEN

NEW TAPE

Lisa: Tell me about the streets – the layout of the town. What were the streets like?

Ruth: Ohhhhh! We'll, the town was laid out in blocks and there were streets going – I've forgotten my directions in relation to the town – I would guess north and south were named after the Presidents. We lived on Jefferson Street. The streets going the opposite way were numbered, 1st, 2nd, 3rd, and 4th. Fourth was the main street of the town. The ships docked at the wharf and we walked up the wharf, right up the main street. And right in front of the bank, which was probably three blocks up from the wharf, in the middle of a green ____ was a tall flagpole with the flag flying from it everyday.

So, you see we were patriotic, even if we were only a territory at that time.

The streets, uh, were dirt. There were a few animals around and I can remember the condition of the middle ____ streets due to horses, sometimes dog teams. There were a few planked streets for pedestrians. Sometimes the planks were lengthwise, maybe a pair of them running lengthwise with a wide crack in between. I was always afraid I would fall through the crack.

Laughter.

And there would be just plain dirt paths to walk on, but…

Lisa: What about the stumps now…?

Ruth: Oh there were stumps everywhere. They made the most wonderful places to play games.

Lisa: They were in the streets?

Ruth: Well, not in the center of the streets, but in between the houses and in the Devil's Club and behind the buildings. The stumps were everywhere. Trees had to be cut down and we didn't have the tools we have nowadays, so they just sawed off the trees and left the stumps.

It's awfully hard to dig out the...

Lisa: We sort of talked about the types of buildings. You said some were two stories. Were they all wood buildings?

Ruth: No, the bank was concrete block. ....

The ..... was wooden, wooden siding. Brown & Hawkins was also a two-story building because over the dry goods section we had the dance hall. You went up an enclosed stairs up to the second floor and there was his dance hall as big as the whole store below – a very nice room as I recall.

Lisa: Now were there many log cabins like ...

Ruth: Yes. There were.

Lisa: What do you remember about the territory and what kind of talk do you recall...

Ruth: The chief thing I remember was constant talk about statehood – there was all that clamor about wanting state status, and that seemed to be the one thing that our politicians were looking for.

Lisa: Do you remember any talk about the big companies that would come in and monopolize the canneries and...were there any canneries in Seward?

Ruth: No.

Lisa: Was there any problem with law and order? That seemed to be a big thing in Skagway when I was reading about Soapy Smith and what an outlawish town that was.

Ruth: Skagway was unique. Not everybody had a Soapy Smith, and the Gold Rush of course made it worse. I'm sure there were problems in Seward, but some way or another they're not what I remember. I don't remember any terrible things like we read in our modern newspapers.

Lisa: I remember you said the bears were tied up outside the jails so you must have had a jail. Did you have a sheriff?

Ruth: Yes, I remember an officer in uniform with a big badge on him, but I've forgotten his name. By the way the jail was only two doors from the church – very convenient – and you remember that's where I had my bears tied up.

Lisa: Was there a mayor that you can remember?

Ruth: Yes I think there was. It would likely be one of the Ballaines (?) but I just can't be sure.

Lisa: Maybe they had a city council? I just wondered if the railroad ran the whole town or?

Ruth: No, the railroad didn't…

Lisa: Joe said that when you first came he thought only three miles of the railroad had been completed and by the time you left they'd gotten to mile 53 or something. Ok, now we'll get off that subject and on to something else.

Lisa: Last time you mentioned the word a comity agreement between the Methodists and Presbyterians and I didn't know what that word meant – I think it's C O M I T Y. Do you know what that means?

Ruth: Well, it's like a gentleman's agreement. It's done in good faith and it's respected and …..

Lisa: That's good. I kind of thought that was what it meant but I didn't know. I don't remember if we ever established how many denominations there were in Seward. I know there was a Lutheran Church that is in a picture that Joe showed me later.

Ruth: Yes, that came in a little later, after we left there. They occupied a building that was right next to the parsonage, which was built after we left there.

Lisa: Yeah he said that – that your Dad's church was on one corner and then there was the house and then right next door to that was the Lutheran Church. So your house was right in between the two…

Ruth: Yes it was, before it burned.

The Lutheran Church was not there when we lived there. There were Episcopal and the Catholic and the Methodist churches in Seward, during our time.

Lisa: I think we have that. I have a picture Joe had that shows your Dad with some Boy Scouts. He must have had a Boy Scout troop.

Ruth: Yes he did.

Lisa: Ok, and that was in Seward?

Ruth: Yes.

Lisa: Did he also have one in Skagway?

Ruth: I don't remember one there. Did Joe mention that Dad taught manual training in the schools in Skagway?

Lisa: No, I really didn't ask him any questions that day. I just felt I shouldn't because of the letter, so I didn't…

Ruth: Dad did teach in the schools in Skagway. He taught manual training and had a very successful class.

Lisa: Ok, now what was there for the kids to do – what did you do besides playing on the stumps? I know I came across something – it might have been a letter Joe wrote when he went back to Alaska – saying that you and he saw the places where you had gone ice-skating. And he also told me about sliding down the roof in the chopping bowl and that the chopping bowl broke. And he told me about Otto Bergstrom taking he and another boy for a weekend.

Ruth: Did he tell you about the rhubarb? It gave them all indigestion. They were tossing and turning in their beds, and outside the owl kept hooting, "Whoo? Whoo?" They hugged each other close all night – they all got a little frightened.

Skating was a great outdoor sport in the wintertime. There were two lakes, First Lake and Second Lake. First Lake was small and really was not used too much. I think it was probably two miles from town. But Second Lake was much larger, farther away, maybe four miles. We thought nothing of hiking out to Second Lake.

Several times during the winter the community would have a community cookout on the banks of the lake and the kids went skating all over the lake. Parents and grandparents, neighbors and friends, would warn them not to get out too far. They'd have a huge bonfire. The packages of meat would be opened up and here would be a package marked "porcupine meat," and the next package would be marked "dog meat" and other packages likewise—various designations. That just added to the fun of the situation.

I can remember we would always be allowed to drink coffee on those occasions, so they'd call all the skaters in and we'd stand around this huge bonfire. There were no environmentalists in those days. We'd have a bowl full of steaming mulligan stew and a cup of coffee in our hands, skates on our feet, and we'd really live it up.

Lisa: Was that really porcupine meat and really dog meat?

Ruth: They never told us. I had my doubts. But if was fun to play with it.

Lisa: What was the source of food – like meat?

Ruth: Much of it was from hunting. Of course one moose would provide quite a bit of meat. People in our family were not hunters, but Dad would always buy a hindquarter of moose in the fall and have it frozen down in the ice house, and then he'd hang it down in our basement in a corner where it would stay frozen all winter, and he'd go down and cut off a piece that we'd need for our meals. We had bear meat. We had ptarmigan. Other wild birds. Snowshoe rabbits.

We had a meat market and occasionally had beef. We used to have eggs – they were cold storage eggs. We had fish too – salmon and halibut, clams. I don't remember oysters. Our oysters were all in oyster stew. I don't remember fried oysters at all. Dad would always put down salmon in a barrel with salt.

Lisa: What about vegetables – did you grow any vegetables?

Ruth: Yes. Potatoes – there was something in the soil, they would turn out to be very sweet, a most peculiar flavor. And the skins were thin with scabs all over the outside and we'd have to peel the potatoes and drain the water. They were perfectly edible but they were scabby potatoes. I can remember in the wintertime sometimes cold weather would get ahead of us and the potatoes we had stored would freeze. I can remember if you took potatoes out to prepare them for dinner, if they were frozen you'd drop them into cold water and the ice would form on the outside of the potatoes, and you'd try to peel them. But they would cook.

But in the summertime we could raise crops for a short time – peas, turnips if the worms didn't get them, some carrots. Oh rhubarb. I've seen rhubarb stalks the size of my arm.

Lisa: What about berries?

Ruth: Yes, wild. Raspberries, black currants, red currants, blueberries, some strawberries. You get down to the area around Haines and that was great strawberry country – huge strawberries.

Lisa: I came across a picture of you and Joe with flowers – looked like wildflowers maybe along the beach.

Ruth: Lots of wildflowers – great meadows of wildflowers, shooting stars, fireweed, which was in great, steep meadows ablaze with fireweed, a very spectacular sight. Mother used to gather fireweed by the tubful, washtub full, and decorate the church.

Lisa: Fireweed is kind of a purple flower isn't it?

Ruth: Reddish purple. And buttercups, daisies, great fields of daisies.

Lisa: Did you have any local artists that would paint pictures?

Ruth: We did, because I remember that Joe showed some ability along that line and there was a woman in Seward who volunteered to give him lessons. She wanted to be a good neighbor so she invited little sister to come along, too, but she didn't take to it, so Joe got all the honors.

Lisa: I think you and I talked about clothes. You said you got a lot of them from Montgomery Ward, and then your Mom made some.

Ruth: Yes and the missionary barrel.

Lisa: Oh really? You had a missionary barrel? Now what's that?

Ruth: Oh, people in the states that felt sorry for those poor little children up there in the north who didn't have any proper clothes. So they would dump all their old clothes into a box and then put them into barrel and ship it up to us. I can remember standing around that barrel and saying, "Oh mama, can I have this? Oh look, I can wear this!"

Laughter.

Maybe mother would pull out an old stained corset or a pair of high-heeled shoes.

Lisa: What about knitted things? Did you knit or did your Mom knit?

Ruth: I don't think my mother ever knitted. She did other types of ...... and she took great pleasure in preparing dainty, pretty things for me. How she had an eye for it I don't know, but I remember one dress in particular made of white linen, with a full skirt, in which there was a deep hem that was hem stitched all the way around, and then above the hem stitching for a distance of about a foot there was what they called shadow embroidery… (Side one ends)

Mother was always doing lovely things like that. When Fred and Ralph went off to school – I mean the university – she sent them out each with a laundry bag, made of ____, one was bound in dark green binding, the other was dark red, their initials were embroidered across the top in old English lettering, there was feather stitching around the binding, *beautifully* done, things of that kind. I don't know how she did it.

Lisa: Well, maybe that was her hobby like your Dad's was photography.

Ruth: There probably wasn't much of anything else to do in the evenings.

Lisa: My next question – what was your Dad's style of preaching? Fundamentalist? Hell fire and brimstone? Because that's the kind of minister I remember from my childhood.

Ruth: Yeah, Dad was fundamentalist. And very emphatic. He'd pound the pulpit once in a while, and I used to sit there and watch him, wondering who was he going to miss? But that was more or less the style in those days. He was dynamic, I'd say.

Lisa: I think I can see him in the swallowtail outfit up there. Ok, next question I've got down here is Indians and Eskimos, and I think you told me there weren't many. You've told me about Billy Lowell.

Ruth: Yes there were not many Indians or Eskimos right in the town itself – they were mostly clustered along the beach in Indian huts that were built up on stilts. I don't think I was ever in one of those homes. I think I told you about my friends that I liked so well, Amy

Birds and Susie Guest. Amy Birds was a half-breed girl, quiet, unassuming, but I loved her very much. She was one of my favorites. The other was Susie Guest; you know the Eskimos are of smaller stature. She was about to my shoulder, and she would look at you with her almost almond-shaped eyes, and you'd see little twinkles coming out of them. Cute little thing. And always anxious to please, always a good sport. I have a picture of my birthday party and those two girls are there.

Lisa: Now the dog teams and the dog sleds we've never gotten into, but it seems to me that that was mentioned once when we were talking as being one of the main forms of travel.

Ruth: Yes I think it was. Have you had time to look at Dr. Reynolds' book? He describes the dog teams most accurately.

Lisa: I'll have to look that up. But he was from a different area – most of that was about the Kuskoquim, and a little bit in the back it mentions Seward. If I'm not mistaken it mentions Seward as being the place where he retired…

Ruth: Yes. But he describes the basket-type sled, which I'm familiar with, and the dog teams, probably eight dogs and the leader. The way the sleds are fitted with fur robes and such as that, and if there were people riding in the sled you know you're not very far above the snow, and you're apt to get pretty cold.

What I remember most about riding in a dog sled was the dogs that let off steam *(laughter)*. You get some awful smells once in a while.

Lisa: I read in another book about Billy Mitchell saying that he fed the dogs better than he fed himself – that he would always make sure his dogs were well fed and that each had an individual bowl so they wouldn't eat one another's food, and the lead dog was always the best dog.

He was the boss and the other dogs knew it.

Lisa: Did you know Billy Mitchell…

Ruth: No.

Lisa: …or know much about him up there? The book I had said he started, I think, made Seward where the underwater telegraph ended…

Ruth: The cable. It went to Seward.

Lisa: Ok, he must have started out there, because he was sent as a trouble-shooter to see why they weren't getting the telegraph cable laid….

When did you get telephone? Was that in Seward?

Ruth: Seward. It would be before 1911 because the news of Willard's birth was phoned to us.

Lisa: Oh, from Valdez.

Ruth: No, it came by cablegram to the office and they phoned to the house. So you see there was the cable.

Lisa: I remember you said when Otto had his bear accident, the bear attacked him, that Dr. Romey (?) called your Dad.

Ruth: Yes.

Lisa: Remember we were talking about the Williwaw winds? That was Seward?

Ruth: Douglas.

Lisa: Seward wasn't in the path of those?

Ruth: No.

Lisa: Was Seward a connecting link to the Iditarod?

Ruth: Yes. I think Mr. Eide, E I D E, carried mail to the Iditarod, so did Mr. Ravel, who was the husband of Eva Lowell, carried mail to these interior towns, and it seems to me it was always by dog team in the wintertime, and the Iditarod I'm sure was part of that itinerary, but whether it was the only way I don't know.

Lisa: What was the weather like? Was it similar in the amount of rain to what we have here?

Ruth: I think probably we had more rain – a lot of rain in Seward. And of course the rain turned to snow in the early fall. I've seen it snow on the 4th of July. My birthday was the last of March and I can remember walking through snow tunnels. The walk would be shoveled out and the snow would be piled on either side, which made it seem higher than it was, and you'd walk through these tunnels to get home from school.

NEW TAPE begins *in mid-thought…*

Ruth: I think Fred's best work was as an executive, perhaps on a more sophisticated level. I hope you won't misunderstand me on that statement, but his work was more of an administrative type and he excelled at it. My Father also had attributes of that kind, but I think he would have felt ill at ease in an office in Philadelphia surrounded by bishops and other executives. Not because they were any better but just because of the rank they had attained. Dad was always self-conscious of his limited education, which I'm sure accounted for some of his feelings.

Dad was always tender towards my mother – he trained the family that deference must be shown toward women. And even in the home he maintained the little social graces – the boys pulling out a chair for their mother. I had to wait a few years before I got that treatment.

They were always trained in women first, caps were doffed to women, and gracious little favors were done for women such as an unexpected flower to wear in their hair, or a little gift on return from a trip. He never forgot.

Another feature of Dad, which I remember so very strongly, is that our evening meal was always one of leisure time. After we were through eating there was always conversation, which we hadn't finished, and we were able to take the time to listen to our Father direct the conversation into current events. The newsmagazine of that day was the old *Literary Digest*, and he would quote from articles in that magazine, and we'd get into discussions. Even the youngest in the family would have an opportunity to participate in it.

And at times there were family devotions. Not always, but that was one of the things that entered into our lives and made a lasting impression. This was around the dinner table. I'm trying to think of things that would help you with Dad's personality. Is it emerging yet?

Lisa: I wish I had known him – he sounds like a really interesting person.

Ruth: He certainly was. And as Willard said, he doesn't know where Dad got the money to buy the books to keep himself informed the way he did. He had a tremendous library and good books – books that stimulated his mind. He'd be off on one subject for a while and then pretty soon he'd be interested in another phase of life or prophecy or history or poetry. He loved poetry, too.

And through it all he took the time to be a good husband and a great father.

Lisa: Now I need to remind you to tell me about Mile point 34 Camp and Billy Lowell.

Ruth: One summer our family and one or two other families joined forces to go on a camping trip out to Mile 34 on the Alaska Central Railroad. There were a couple of men who were hunters, Billy Lowell, the half-breed Indian, was our guide and main hunter. A hand-pumped handcar was our means of locomotion, and that was a great morning when all of the gear was piled onto the handcar. We youngsters were allowed to sit on the edge with our feet hanging over, while the men took turns pumping that car for 34 miles to get out where the campsite had been chosen.

Before leaving town Mr. Shaw, the editor of the paper, came to my folks and said that he was concerned about them going out to Mile 34 in the hill country and bear country with no more protection than these hunters. He said he would feel better if we had a dog with us who knew how to handle bears. So he wanted to lend us his dog Prince to take and keep with us as long as we were on our camping trip. Now Prince was a beautiful big Great Dane and Prince came along – he understood that he was our dog for a few days and I don't recall whether he rode or hiked all that distance. I kind of think he hiked a good ways.

We get out to Mile 34 and the men pitch the tents and the mothers made up the beds. Everybody fixed a little fire in front of the tents to make the evening meal. I can remember my mother making baking powder biscuits and cooking them over the bonfire in what they call a little reflector – they were awfully good. That night we were visited by porcupines. Prince didn't think that was very funny so he scrounged into the tent with the rest of us.

The next morning the hunters went out to see if they could find any signs of bear and pretty soon one of them came back and said he found the bear tracks – *"We're going out to get a bear,"* so everybody was all excited. Prince stood up on his four legs and his tail went up in the air – he looked a little suspicious but he went with the hunters and with the men of the camp, trailing that bear. They followed his tracks through the shrubs and through the bushes and finally came to a clearing, which was muddy, and the first thing they knew, here ahead was some mud that was still steaming. They knew they were right on the heels of the bear, and Prince went forward and smelled that footprint in the mud and his tail went down with a bang between his legs and his head went down almost touching his two front feet and he headed back for the camp.

And when the hunters got back – with the bear – where was Prince? Nobody knew. Prince had absolutely disappeared. They couldn't find Prince anywhere. They didn't know what to do – they couldn't find him. They were sure the bears hadn't gotten him. But when we got into town we learned that Prince had started back to town and never stopped till he got home again.

LOUIS AND FANNY

Mr. Shaw apologized for his dog's bad manners.

Here was the great, big dog that was to protect all of us.

But the interesting story is the trip that my father and mother took to New York. Every summer there was the tourist trade up the coast of Alaska. And one summer among the tourists were a group from New York City. George W. Perkins and his wife, his sister and Mrs. Brewster, and others in the party. George Perkins was a secretary to J.P. Morgan if I have my history straight – I think I do. Anyway he was a man of some means and active in missionary work. They had heard of the work that was being done in Seward and, as part of their mission in taking this tourist trip, they wanted to see the work that was being carried on.

They were in port for two or three days and during that time the Perkins party and my Father and Mother became fast friends. Mr. Perkins learned of my father's desire to establish a YMCA in Seward for the benefit of the single men, chiefly, who had no place to go – no recreation available to them except the saloons. Dad felt that if there were only a YMCA that was clean and modestly furnished it would provide something for these single men that would be desirable.

So arrangements were made that my Father would take his sabbatical leave, which was due him, and I don't know what the financial arrangements were, but I do know that the Perkins helped my parents finance the trip. It became quite an event in our family. It was the year 1909, when the Alaska Yukon Pacific Exposition was being held in Seattle. So my Mother, brother Joe and I came out first and stopped in Seattle to attend the fair, and that was a great time in our lives. Then we were joined I think about three months later by my Father and two older brothers. We were taken to Salem, Oregon, where Fred and Ralph were placed in the Willamette Academy. They were living in a private home. My brother Joe and I were domiciled in another private home and placed in grade school in Salem while my folks went back to New York City, I suppose by train, and in New York City they stayed in the home of the George W. Perkins family.

While there, my Dad gave illustrated lectures on Alaska. He would dress in a fur parka and mukluks and walk down the streets of New York City carrying a banner which said, "All About Alaska – See the Beautiful Pictures." The banner would tell where it was and what time. He would often be followed by a string of dogs sniffing at his mukluks and looking just a little bit cowed at the smell that emanated, but his lectures were well attended and the money came in from somewhere. I think there was a collection taken – something of that kind – but they were well attended and created a great deal of interest.

Lisa: Now were these talks the ones that had the lanternslides that he had colored with oils?

Ruth: Yes. Yes. Pictures that he had taken himself and he made the slides himself, and then he colored them and protected them, too.

Lisa: What were the mukluks and parkas made of that they smelled?

Ruth: Some kind of fur that had probably been in an Eskimo hut for a long time – picked up a little Eskimo smell.

Mr. Perkins himself was a heavy contributor to the YMCA project. Enough money was raised that upon return from New York they picked up their family in Salem, Oregon, and we all journeyed back to Alaska on the Alameda, as I recall.

Dad purchased a rather large building that was right on the edge of the beach, just opposite where the boats landed, and established a very acceptable YMCA and I will show you the picture…

Lisa: Now did your Dad run the YMCA?

Ruth: He did. He had a caretaker living there, Brother Bill, who lived upstairs, and he was the caretaker and kept the place clean. He maintained order so there was no rowdyism, and it was well patronized by the community.

Lisa: Now did the YMCA have room for men to sleep?

Ruth: I think there were one or two rooms but not to the extent that our modern YMCA's have.

Lisa: Now just to make sure I have it straight, Mrs. Brewster was Mrs. Perkins' sister?

Ruth: That's my understanding, yes. You might be interested to know that this family maintained their interest and their contacts with the Pedersen family over a period of many years and made substantial gifts, usually at Christmastime or some other time when they just felt the urge for it.

Mrs. Brewster, especially, remembered Joe and Ruth. About the time that I graduated from 8th grade she sent me a ring with three small diamonds in it and about a year later she sent me a ring with a square-cut emerald with a diamond on either side of the emerald. And that was really something for a poor little missionary girl way up there in Alaska. She stipulated that I was to have them at the present time and enjoy wearing them, and that when the time came for my education I was to use them for that purpose if I needed the money.

Lisa: And did you?

Ruth: No. One of the rings was stolen and the other one I still have.

Lisa: Which one?

Ruth: Well, this one.

Lisa: Oh that's the one with the three—

Ruth: Two. Two diamonds. Originally there were three when she sent it to me but these are the two stones.

Lisa: And you had them reset?

Ruth: Yes.

Lisa: Pretty diamonds.

Ruth: They were old-fashioned mountings. I wish I hadn't had them changed, but I did.

There were other gifts she sent from time to time, too. But those gifts were so unique that there was an article about their arrival in the Skagway paper. Nowadays we wouldn't think of putting it in the paper.

Lisa: You're referring to the rings?

Ruth: Yes, and there was a watch, a key-wind watch, in solid gold case which came also. I had always thought it was sent to my brother Joe directly, but he thinks it was sent to my Father and Father passed it on to him.

So that's the story of the YMCA – another one of Dad's projects.

Remember I told you that the churches had frequent socials and events that were community-wide. One time there was a Japanese event where the Japanese members of the community came in and cooked some Japanese delicacies, if that's the right word for it, but the Church was decorated with Japanese knickknacks, and the women of the town really outdid themselves in dressing appropriately. My mother made me a little Japanese outfit, made especially for the occasion, and we were fortunate in finding yardage that had the Japanese weave in it, so she made the little kimono with the wide sash. I don't know where she got the umbrella but I guess it was available there.

This is the outfit she made for me.

Lisa: You must have been about 10 in the picture?

Ruth: I don't think I was any more than that.

Lisa: Was this the kind of affair where your Dad would print up posters and put them around town?

Ruth: He might, yes. Or there might be a meeting of the literary society where they would meet and discuss a book or there might be a ...

Lisa: Did he have anything to do with the Literary Society?

Ruth: Yes, he was the genesis of it. They would pick out books to study and someone would give a report on it and they would discuss it. Just a brainteaser type of thing.

And of course there was the Ladies Aid and the young Girls Aid society. I don't recall any musical groups.

Lisa: Who taught you piano?

Ruth: I started piano in Seward from a local lady. Joe started at the same time. Joe's hands and mine are very different. His hand is kind of square with short fingers and I had no trouble reaching the wide stance. He had a great deal of trouble. One day the teacher said in desperation, *"Joe, I'm going to get a knife and cut right down them so you have more room."* That was the end of Joe's lessons – he never took another lesson after that. He refused. And I think Joe could have learned to play, but that was that.

Lisa: That was in Seward?

Ruth: Yes, in Seward I learned enough to start playing hymns. Then after we moved to Skagway the folks found another teacher for me and I really made good progress in Skagway.

Then after we came out I studied for several years under Professor Marcus in Seattle and I really made good progress.

Lisa: Now were you going to pursue a career in music, Ruth? I think I heard once that you did teach piano.

Ruth: Yes I did, I taught piano for several years. After my marriage broke up I went down to Raymond where the Wahlstroms lived, took an apartment there and set up a little studio, and had a class of about 50 pupils there. They were in South Bend. I did very well.

Then I went back to my husband to ____ for a while, so I gave up my classes down there, which was a mistake, because the second try didn't go either, so after that I taught in Bellingham, a nice little class there …

Lisa: Now did you teach like a group lesson, or…

Ruth: It was individual lessons and then they would meet as a group about once a month and we would put on a semi-recital, which some hated, some loved. They organized themselves into the Musicland Club and got attention in the newspaper.

Lisa: Now did you ever finish college?

Ruth: No.

Lisa: You never did.

Ruth: No.

Lisa: Have you regretted that?

Ruth: Yes. I would like to have finished college – sure would. Many reasons.

Lisa: Can you tell me now a little bit about your Mom, uh, I've been trying to put myself into her shoes and I'm having difficulty because of the difference in environments that she must have experienced.

Ruth: Well, she was rather a small person of Pennsylvania Dutch extraction. She was third in a family of 10 children and accustomed to…

NEW TAPE

LOUIS AND FANNY

Lisa: Ruth, I can't imagine getting all the information about Louie and the family without also getting information about Fanny. I have great difficulty putting myself in Fanny's shoes going from a comfortable residence – or semi-comfortable, whatever it was – on Douglas Island and then going into a tent with four kids. I think she must have been quite a lady.

Ruth: Well I think you have said the right thing. It's hard to imagine my Mother without putting my Father with her – because the two were inseparable. Although, at times words apart, too. I recall mother as being rather a small person with shiny brown eyes that twinkled, a quick smile, and a gracious way of looking out for her kids and her family. She was always at my Dad's side supporting him with decisions, some of which were reached after discussions that I can recall might have been a little heated at times. Because mother was an independent thinker. And I heard her say a time or two with a twinkle in her eye that, *"Louie,"* as she called my father, *"thinks he's the businessman but he needs a little straightening out once in a while."*

Lisa: Good for Fanny.

Ruth: Yes. He doesn't know that I know that.

I think she was a woman who was dedicated to her calling. I do not recall ever hearing her complain about the conditions under which we lived in Seward for a time. She was a determined little person, expecting obedience from her children and at the same time reassuring them and making the whole adventure a game so that we didn't feel that we were underprivileged in any way.

Living turned into a lark when we would stand at the table in the tent, or sit on a hardwood bench with hot rocks under our feet to keep warm, or a fur cap to keep our ears warm, a coat around us, mittens on our fingers. The fun might have been to see who would get through first and get into the shanty where it was a little warmer. I don't recall how we did dishes in those days – there were no paper dishes, I know that – but she and Dad had it worked out some way or other. We were all taken care of and nobody felt put upon.

As a child growing up into a teenager at the age when you like to bring your companions home for an evening meal or a class party or just some little waif that was alone, afraid to be left alone while her mother was away, our home was always open. *"Sure, bring her on in, that's all right. We'll find an extra piece of meat. Just set a place for her at the table."* Or, if there was to be a party, Ruth would always pipe up, "Well, can they come to the parsonage?" Yes that was all right, too. Maybe they wouldn't get much to eat but usually there was something – at least canned milk ice cream – and that was good.

Every Thursday as I recall was calling day and Mother would dress in her nice skirt, pretty blouse, hat and jacket, and Father would dress in his best business suit, which was probably his only business suit, and go calling. And that was the day that, as I grew older, I would start making supper in the evening. And my mother would smile and she'd say, *"Well, Louie, I can bank on one thing."* What's that? *"Well, we'll have dessert for supper tonight if we have nothing else."* So her humor showed through, every so often.

Particularly when we had younger brothers in the family there wasn't quite so much time to make dessert – there were faces to be washed for dinner and other preparations to make.

Mother was very interested in the work of the Women's Christian Temperance Union and became a territorial officer – I believe she was treasurer – a position she held for many years, and as a territorial officer she made a couple of trips Outside to regional meetings of the organization. In fact her position was so publicly stated and she let it be known emphatically of her belief in this matter that her name is quoted in a book on Skagway and she is listed as Mrs. L.H. Pedersen of Skagway, Alaska. You know I smiled to think that it was she who got her name immortalized in a book and rather than our Father.

Lisa: What's the name of the book, do you know?

Ruth: That's the book I asked you to get from Joe. Roby gave Joe that book. I don't know the name of it. He showed it to me once. Willard happened to see it in the bookstore at the University among books on Alaska – it stood out, he was just thumbing through it, and all of a sudden that name stuck out, Mrs. L.H. Pedersen. And he recognized it.

Lisa: I wish I knew what the book was.

Ruth: Well, Joe will know. It's a fairly recent book and it's about the history of Skagway.

Transcriber's note: I believe it's The Skagway Story, a paperback by Howard Clifford, published in 1975 by Alaska Northwest Books of Seattle, Anchorage and Portland. I found the ninth printing (1997) in the University Bookstore in about 1998. Mrs. L.H. Pedersen and the activities of the Alaska WCTU are discussed on pages 159-161. Editorial offices of Alaska Northwest Books are at 2208 NW Market Street, Suite 300, Seattle 98107, phone (800) 452-3032.

Lisa: Now was this all in Skagway when she was active in the WCTU?

Ruth: No, it began in Seward. I don't know whether – it might have been in Douglas too or not – but during the time we lived in Seward she was visited by a national officer of the WCTU, Mrs. Jewett, who liked Alaska so well she stayed and became Mrs. Hatcher (?). She stayed in our home for several weeks and because of Mother's affiliation my next brother, just younger than I am, was named Willard after Frances Willard, the founder of WCTU. That's where he got his name. So there's a direct relationship. And because of that designation two little souvenirs were sent to my Mother from Frances Willard's home – I believe it's Evanston, Illinois. There was a sugar shell, a very dainty one in the shape of an oak leaf bowl, and I think the other item was a butter knife but they're from the home and personal collection of Frances Willard and of course they are now my brother's possession.

Lisa: That's wonderful.

Ruth: I'm trying to think of some other things that would be helpful. Do you have any questions?

Lisa: The one thing that came into my mind when you were talking of eating in the tent was that you wore a hat and gloves and coat – did you leave the gloves on when you ate, too?

Ruth: Well, (laughter), that detail I don't know. The gloves were so much a part of you that you didn't think about them. I recall that usually when we went outside we pulled knitted gloves on over our hands first and then on top of that mittens, which gave us a double layer and were warmer than a heavy item of any one kind. No I think we at least pulled our gloves off.

Our fur caps were interesting. They were built in a triangle that met at the center on top, sewn together and folded up to expose our ears, weather permitting or, if you wanted you could cover your ears and cover your eyes. There was a bill in front, fur covered, to protect us from cold too. Each one of us had our own fur cap – it was just, just a part of us.

I think I mentioned I was so accustomed to dressing up before going I went out of the house that the night our house burned I took time to get properly attired before I went.

Lisa: Yes….we giggled over that one. You were out there ringing the (fire) bell a long time.

(Faint, garbled conversation – something about what they did after their house burned).

Ruth: It's a good thing I did because I was out there a long time. Joe was talking when he was here…oh he mentioned we stayed at one of the hotels for about a week and when they got the burned area boarded up we lived on the first floor while they worked above us, and then the time came when we went back to our rooms, and at night we'd hear noises and think it was the fire again. We'd have bad dreams or nightmares. It was a traumatic experience.

I remember that at one some of the boards were charred on the outside but ok on the inside, and they were left…and at night we would smell the fire. I used to wonder if it didn't bother our folks as much as it did us children.

Mother particularly enjoyed friendship with Mrs. Korth in Seward. Mrs. Korth – K O R T H – was a Russian lady, right from Russia, who had been part of the Russian occupation. She was of the Greek Orthodox religion, but she and mother formed an intimate friendship and once a week they would have tea together. Mother was not a tea drinker but she looked forward to these little afternoon social times together and there were several children, the one I remember chiefly is Peter. Peter was a little older than I, and I have a brother who always insisted that Peter was out to (look for?) me, but he was a nice boy and there was Eunith Korth and Esther Korth – all of them raised in the Russian tradition. Mrs. Korth had a samovar that she used to make tea, and to go into their home was quite an experience because they had many of the original Russian…I don't know, not antiques but choice pieces of china and accessories. They were very lovely folks.

Lisa: Now did they go then to the Russian church?

Ruth: There was no Russian church in Seward at that time. I think the Russian priest came in at intervals to hold services.

I've often wondered when Mother and Dad went down to the first dance at the dance hall there, I wonder what Mother's thoughts were, if she didn't kind of wish that she was out there gliding across the floor. I'm sure she had thoughts of that kind because she was a very attractive person. I remember one time she and I were together and I said, *"Mama, my tongue is sore. I have a sore spot on my tongue,"* and she said, *"You must have been telling a lie."* I looked at her and said, *"How did you know?"* She said, *"Well, it showed on your face."*

She was quick – I couldn't get ahead of her.

From time to time we as children were ill. There were certain things that were special. If we were ill we could have a piece of canned pineapple to tempt our appetites – otherwise it was almost a forbidden fruit because it was so expensive. Or we could have spears of white asparagus. It came in square pans that un-winded around the top. It was a special invitation to eat also. There were certain little things of that kind that knew we could have when we were ill. And it kind of helped to get over it.

Then there were the days of the 1918 flu. We had just come out of Alaska. Six of us came down with flu at one time.

Lisa: All six kids?

Ruth: Uh, four kids, five kids and the grandmother. Mother was the only one who was not down with the flu. And how she went from one sick person to another taking care...and we were all just quite ill, and she was up day and night looking after us. Finally her older sister came from Raymond to stay with us.

Lisa: You mentioned Grandmother. I hate to intrude on Fanny. But Grandmother Olson stayed in Alaska for any length of time?

Ruth: Not very long. She came – I don't recall the year – came to us in Skagway and I think she lived there less than two years when we came out.

Lisa: I remember one picture – you said she lived in a little house sort of behind the church.

Ruth: Yes, she came into our home and we didn't have a really adequate place for her in the Presbyterian manse. Now here's where this comity arrangement came in. We were living in the Presbyterian manse and this small house behind the church was the Methodist parsonage and we had the use of both of them.

The Methodist parsonage was very small – little tiny... Dad had set up his study and office over there – I remember that well – so after Grandmother had been with us for a while in the manse it became evident that she would be happier by herself. She wasn't used to children...(gap) and strangers coming in and disrupting things. So the folks fixed her up over there and she was very comfortable. She could continue with her vice over there.

LOUIS AND FANNY

Lisa: Did she continue living with your Dad after that?

Ruth: Yes. Yes until she died.

Lisa: How long was she...?

Ruth: Well, she died in about ...twenty-seven.

Lisa: Oh wow, so she lived quite a while after Fanny. Did she live with Marion then and your Dad?

Ruth: Yes. And that was quite a _____ experience, too.

Lisa: Was she ever senile or anything?

Ruth: Oh yes. (Audio very faint) She was senile to the extent that she was dangerous. They found her secreting butcher knives...

Lisa: Oh no...

Ruth: ... and such, long pointed scissors, things of that kind. They finally barred her room – they nailed some slats across her door because they were afraid to have her downstairs. (Audio fades out)....And they did that while they were waiting for (tape fades out).....Dad had her committed to Sedro-Woolley...and I heard him tell how when they went through the gates to go in there she turned to him and said ..... said she just couldn't hardly take it. She wasn't there very long before she died. But that was pretty rough on our family.

Lisa: Oh no. Was she ever able to help Fanny when....?

Ruth: No and after Mother died she wanted to help me. And she meant it. She was just as confused as she could be, but Daddy had put his foot down and told her, "No, Mother, you're not to be in charge of the kitchen" – just let her know that I was...

She would help me. She could peel potatoes, she could peel other vegetables and do things like that, but we couldn't trust her with turning on the heat to the stove…

She would help with the washing and straightening and she would come in…and she would do dishes endlessly if we would let her. But her aprons were used for handkerchiefs and she'd pick up a dish and dry it with her apron – you just had to watch continually. One day she took all the good silver and decided she wanted to make sure it was dry. She put it all in the oven and didn't tell anybody and she forgot it, so about three days went by before it was discovered where the good silver was.

And it was ___ handled so it was melted into the joints there …. (Fades out).

I never knew too much about Mother's early life. She came from a family of 10 children, she was third in the family, evidently a hard-working family, intelligent people. They came from Indiana across the United States to the Pacific Coast settling in the Willapa Harbor country. They lived in Oysterville, Bay Center, that area. Her father at one time was sheriff of Pacific County and postmaster at South Bend. He died at a fairly young age of a heart attack. The family were all of them interested in forestry and the most outstanding one was Will Turner who was associated with Willapa Lumber Company, which eventually was taken over by Weyerhaeuser.

Lisa: Was Cora her sister?

Ruth: Yes. Mother was third in the family. Cora was ninth. She had a younger sister, Jesse, who died when she was 19 and that was of TB.

We were talking about my mother. I've heard her refer to teaching school sometime before she was married. I'm not sure where this occurred – I do know that she worked as a hired girl I guess they called it in those days for a family in Astoria because that's where she met Dad.

I've heard her tell how her "master of the home" brought home a watermelon and she wasn't used to watermelon and didn't know what to do with it so she boiled it.

Laughter.

They had a lot of fun kidding her about that one – she put it in the wash water. I can't imagine anyone would want that.

Lisa: That's cute. She was 19 when they married? I've gotten a few glimpses going back over the tapes of things I think she must have instilled in the kids….

END OF TAPE

Appendix 5

The Pedersen Heritage in Wrangell

Louis and Fanny Pedersen never lived in Wrangell, but the town played a remarkable role in the family story and was the focus of several coincidences.

As the Pedersens traveled north in 1903 to their first assignment in Douglas, their steamship followed the sheltered Inside Passage route of today's Alaska Ferries. It was clear they were leaving behind the civilization they'd known in Astoria, Portland and Salem, Oregon. Hour after hour passed with no settlements and no people. Hours stretched into days.

The landscape emphasized the frontier – steep mountains, dense forests, misty channels. Great waterfalls zigzagged down sheer cliffs in a series of long runs to the sea. It's much the same today – primitive, powerful, unknowable.

Louis and Fanny surely were looking forward to a mail and freight stop in Wrangell, and no doubt knew its history well. Just decades earlier Wrangell had been a Russian fur post at the mouth of the Stikine River. It's where the Presbyterians established the first Protestant foothold in Alaska in 1878, where the renowned missionary Sheldon Jackson fought his first battles against the evils of alcohol.

Decades after the Pedersens came north, their son Joe would marry a woman, Mildred Pederson (with an "o"), whose brother Russell was the Presbyterian minister here in the 1930s, and who later would become Presbyterian minister at Louis's church in Skagway. And

LOUIS AND FANNY

Louis and Fanny's son Willard would marry a young Seattle schoolteacher who lived and worked in Wrangell at the same time as Russell, long before the two women married Pedersen brothers.

Helen described how townspeople in those days watched the horizon for smoke above the island called Elephant's Nose. "When you saw smoke, you know a boat was coming and looked forward to collecting mail at the post office," she said. "A line would form immediately. Those who weren't waiting for mail boarded the boat to dance to the ship's orchestra, and the travelers would 'do the town.'"

Helen graduated from the University of Washington in 1934 with a degree in Public School Education and a major in music and English. This was during the Depression when jobs were scarce and salaries were poor. An offer of $1,450 a year to teach in Wrangell was far superior to the $1,250 she could earn at home.

Helen tells of arriving here "on a gray day, in a gray town, with a gray hotel near a gray dock." She adjusted to the gloom and as time went along, "I found myself responsible for many things in the community."

Helen taught music from kindergarten through 12th grade to about 125 students, and also played the organ for the Catholic, Episcopal and Presbyterian churches, and had about 15 piano students. The churches staggered their services so Helen could play at all three every Sunday.

Appendix 6

Pedersens in *The Skagway Daily Alaskan*

Oct. 1916 – Dec. 1918

Compiled and paraphrased by Richard F. Pedersen, son of Ralph Pedersen and former U.S. ambassador to Hungary and the United Nations, and president of The American University of Cairo. Dick became interested in the period when his dad was editor of the Skagway newspaper. These summaries provide a revealing glimpse into everyday life within the Pedersen family and the Skagway community.

10-14-16 Personals. Ralph Pedersen will arrive in Skagway on the *Alice* next Wednesday. Mr. Pedersen will spend the winter assisting his father in his photographic work.

10-18-16. The Canadian Pacific steamer *Alice* arrived here at eight o'clock this morning with a fair passenger list... It is about 12 hours of its schedule. The Skagway passengers on the big boat are... Ralph M. Pedersen.

10-21-16 The Week in Society. Mr. Ralph Pedersen returned on the *Princess Alice* from a trip to Seattle. Mr. Pedersen will engage in photography with brother and father. Church Notes: (Sunday Services) The Wonderful Paul. (Evening Talk) Unsatisfied Religious CURIOSITY. L.H. Pedersen, Minister (Presbyterian Church in the Methodist Hall)

10-26-16 Page 1 banner headline: Wedding bells merrily jingled last evening when Rev. L.H. Pedersen joined J.M. Keller, popular publicity man of the Garden City, and Miss Myrtle A. Lindsay, of Seattle, in the bonds of holy matrimony. (Long article. Keller was son of the newspaper's publisher.)

10-28-16 Church Notes. Rev. L.H. Pedersen went to Haines on the Petrson (sic) this afternoon to hold services Sunday. (Local minister away.)

10-30-16 Temperance Program. The Temperance Institute . . . will be held tomorrow . . . at the Methodist Church. (Program) . . . Closing remarks: Mrs. L.H. Pedersen.

10-31-16 Court House Instruments. Release of Tax Lien from L.H. Pedersen to J.D. Matlock.

11-2-16 Note saying W.E. Burford, editor of the paper, had retired.

11-22-16 Skagway School News. The fourth room gave a very interesting program last Friday morning. A Dialogue (That Dreadful Boy) was especially good. Characters were: ... Mr. Ford – Joseph Pedersen. Girls of Miss Benthien's room organized a basketball team: ... Ruth Pedersen.

12-4-16 Pedersen Bros. Store. Your chance to purchase neatly made, plain and fancy aprons, and embroidered articles for your Xmas giving, at reasonable prices.

12-6-16 School Notes (contains story by Ruth Pedersen, Ninth Grade) "Eppie brings love to a miner." (6 paragraphs)

12-11-16 (two column wide ad with large type, fancy heading. HOLIDAY GIFTS AT PEDERSEN BROTHERS STORE. Includes Royal albums of all sizes, hand colored enlargements, complete photo printing outfits, artistic calendars, Christmas cards, films, film albums, supplies, etc. Store Open Until 9 pm.

12-18-16 (Long editorial in which Keller, who has been away in the fall, fires the person left in charge of the paper on the grounds of sensationalism and citing allegations of being pro-German)

12-20-16 A Twice Told Tale (story of a Captain and a boy on a ship

DAN PEDERSEN

by Ruth F. Pedersen, 3 paragraphs)

12-30-16 The Rev and Mrs. L.H. Pedersen entertained on Christmas for a number of their friends . . . (included Ralph, Ruth, Joseph, Willard, Andrew)

Full text: The Reverend and Mrs. L.H. Pedersen entertained on Christmas for a number of their friends. The hostess was assisted by Miss Marjorie Brown. Miss Brown prepared the place cards and helped with the table and room decorations. The table was centered by a pot of ferns and beautiful with other decorations of holly and ribbons. A veritable feast was spread and a delightful afternoon and evening spent in the Pedersen's home. Those present were Mr. and Mrs. G.V. Vinkan, Miss Elizabeth Benthien, Miss Marjorie Brown, Mr. Hermann Olson, Mr. Ralph Pedersen, Miss Ruth Pedersen, Mr. Joe Pedersen, Masters Willard and Andrew Pedersen, and the host and hostess, the Reverend and Mrs. Pedersen.

1-6-17 The Week in Society. Mr. Ralph Pedersen has been added to the Skagway Daily Alaskan force and promises to "make good" in the reportorial department.

1-9-17 Local Briefs. A cable message was received today saying that Fred L. Pedersen, son of Rev. and Mrs. L.H. Pedersen, recently took sick from kidney trouble and was taken from his home in Pe Ell to a hospital in Seattle. He's now reported as doing well and expects to return to his work shortly.

1-17-17 Ralph Pedersen, who accepted a position with the Daily Alaskan on Jan. 2 as local news reporter, is confined to his home with what appears to be pleurisy. Mr. Pedersen attended the basket ball game last Friday night at the white Pass club and seemed to be in excellent health but during the night the attack came on and Saturday morning he was suffering excruciating pain, since which time he has been confined to his bed. Today his father, Rev. Pedersen, states that he is somewhat improved but still unable to be about.

1-24-17 (front page) Skagway Alpine Club Organizes. Responding to the invitation extended by the Tuesday Hike Club, through the medium of Rev. L.H. Pedersen's article appearing in yesterday's impression of this paper, thirty-six persons were present at the

Presbyterian lecture room last evening when Miss Agnes Moffett, president of the Tuesday Hike Club, called the meeting to order. (Reorganized as The Skagway Alpine Club.) President: L.H. Pedersen. Members included all old Tuesday Hike Club members, including: Ruth Pedersen, Joseph Pedersen, Ralph Pedersen, Mrs. L.H. Pedersen, L.H. Pedersen.

1-27-17 Ralph Pedersen is rapidly convalescing from the severe attack of pleurisy, which has confined him to his home for the past several weeks and it is reported he will soon be able to be out. Church Notes: Owing to sickness in the minister's family, there will be no preaching services tomorrow morning and evening.

1-31-17 Honor Roll for the semester (90%) Joseph Pedersen, Ruth Pedersen.

2-6-17 Skagway Alpine Club. (Renewed meeting to take place on constitution, etc., article signed by L.H. Pedersen. Previously was long editorial in favor of the club.)

2-10-17 The Week in Society. A letter to the Reverend and Mrs. L.H. Pedersen sates that their son, the Reverend Fred Pedersen, is convalescing from typhoid fever in the Seattle General Hospital and that he will soon be able to return to his field of labor at Pe Ell, Wash. ... Mr. Ralph Pedersen is again out and will soon be in his usual good health.

2-15-17 Alpine Club. (Lecture Tuesday, Feb. 20, at Popular Picture Palace. L.H. Pedersen lecturing . . . using 125 colorful photo slides of Yellowstone National Park. (Not his)

2-21-17 (Strong editorial in favor of Alpine Club. Article on the meeting saying L.H. Pedersen had read material on Yellowstone in a distinct and easy manner.) Washington's birthday tomorrow. Closing at noon: Pedersen Bros.

3-6-17 Fred Pedersen and wife, according to advice received in this city on one of the last mail steamers, will return to the north on the 17th of this month and take up their residence here for the summer. Mr. Pedersen will take charge of the photographic dark room of Pedersen Bros., and it is the intention of the Pedersen Brothers to vacate the small building just south of the Presbyterian Church as a workroom and move into the second story of their store building on Broadway. Mr. and Mrs. Fred Pedersen will reside in the cottage thus vacated, which will be put in shape for them shortly after their arrival here . . . Ralph Pedersen has received an offer from the White Pass to enter its service during the coming season. The position offered is with the Yukon River division of the system.

3-10-17 Silver Medal Contest. Skagway Branch of the WCTU. Six contestants, including Ruth Pedersen.

3-17-17 The Reverend Fred Pedersen and his young wife arrived on the *Princess Sophia* and will make their home for the summer in Skagway. The young couple will occupy the Methodist parsonage on Main St., between Fourth and Fifth Avenues. Mr. Pedersen is the son of the Reverend and Mrs. L.H. Pedersen and has come north to fully recover from the severe illness, which confined him to his room the greater part of the winter. Mr. Pedersen was appointed pastor of the Methodist church at Pe Ell, Washington, which position he filled up to the time of his illness.

3-17-17 The earlier part of this week, Mr. Ralph Pet(sic)ersen entertained the Washington "U" Club at the home of his parents, the Reverend and Mrs. L.H. Pedersen. The evening was very pleasantly passed with college songs, instrumental music, recalling the bygone days and last but not least a delicious supper. Those present were (7 people) plus Mr. Joseph Pedersen, the host Mr. Ralph Pedersen and his parents the Reverend and Mrs. L.H. Pedersen.

3-24-17 The Week in Society. Mrs. Fred Pedersen was given a reception on Wednesday afternoon by the Women's Church Auxiliary at the home of the Reverend and Mrs. L.H. Pedersen. Mrs. Pedersen received a cordial welcome as nearly three score ladies called to greet her to her home in the northland where she will be for the season. Delicious refreshments were served throughout the afternoon. . . . On Monday evening the Washington "U" club gave the Reverend Fred Pedersen and his young wife a very pleasant surprise by getting together at the residence of the Reverend and Mrs. L.H. Pedersen where the young couple are visiting. A happy evening was enjoyed with music, both instrumental and vocal, and many

LOUIS AND FANNY

stories of university days were told. The guests and members of the Pedersen household enjoyed a delicious supper.

3-29-17 (front page) The First Presbyterian Church of Skagway Organizes Today. Rev. David Waggoner, Stated Clerk, (and others listed) are here to complete the organization of the Presbyterian Church this evening starting at 7:30. (Three years ago the Presbyterian, Episcopal and Methodist Churches asked one church to send a minister to Skagway for 3 years. The Methodist Episcopal Church did, ending Sept. 30 last. Members of the Presbytery came last summer and recommended that the Presbyterian Church start out Oct. 1. That was done, "Mr. Pedersen continuing as minister for one year." The present organization is the completing of those plans.

3-30-17 First Presbyterian Church of Skagway organized last evening with a charter list of 42 members. The Week in Society. On Thursday afternoon a little informal gathering was held at the Presbyterian manse which included the entire family of the Reverend L.H. Pedersen and the visitors from various stations in the Presbytery (Ministers listed from Homa, Juneau, Wrangell, Haines) . . . The Rev and Mrs. Fred Pedersen are now at home to their friends in the Methodist parsonage on Main Street between Fourth and Fifth Avenues. Church Notes. Rev. L.H. Pedersen will leave for Haines on the Spokane to be gone most of the week. (The Presbytery was meeting there.)

4-4-17 Rev. L.H. Pedersen received 1 vote for Mayor.

4-6-17 Declaration of war voted and signed by Wilson.

4-12-17 On Monday morning at assembly Mr. Ralph Pedersen gave a talk on the University of Washington. His talk had 3 separate divisions: Why we should go to a university, what a university is, and how one can go to a university. The talk was very interesting and contained much good advice to grammar grade and high school pupils who intend to go to an institution of higher learning.

4-13-17 Medal Contest Program (WCTU) Group II: Song . . . Willard Pedersen (and others) Mr. Rooster & Mr. Hen.

4-14-17 Medal Contest Program, Group 1: Song . . . The Ginger Cat .

DAN PEDERSEN

. . Willard Pedersen (also II same as above).

5-1-17 Home Guard Organized. Those who signed: . . . Fred L. Pedersen, Ralph M. Pedersen, L.H. Pedersen. (Benediction and opening prayers at meeting by L.H. Pedersen. 76 enroll for home defense.)

5-2-17 Re Alpiners meeting: Pres L.H. Pedersen announced a hike schedule.)

5-3-17 Home guard up to 93 and now organized.

5-9-17 Mr. Pedersen giving manual training guidance in school.

5-10-17 Home guard up to 100.

5-12-17 Alaska Women's Patriotic League. 17 members in Skagway including Mrs. L.H. Pedersen.

5-16-17 The Rev. L. H. Pedersen left last night on the Spokane for Astoria, where his mother lives. It is the first time he has been "outside" in seven years. Instead of taking a long vacation, as he had planned to do, he will return about June 1 to resume the duties that attend him here. His mother will come with him, to make her home here.

6-4-17 The Rev. L.H. Pedersen, pastor of the Presbyterian church, returned on the Sophia from Astoria, Ore., where he had been the past few weeks. He was accompanied by Mrs. J.M. Olsen, his mother, who will make her home here. The Week in Society. The Reverend L.H. Pedersen returned recently from a visit to Astoria, Oregon, where he visited with his mother Mrs. (Captain) J.M. Olsen. Mrs. Olsen returned with her son and will make her home with his family.

6-23-17 On June 14, 1916 were born in the White Pass hospital three little boys, Andrew Pedersen, son of the Reverend L.H. Pedersen . . . and (others). Mothers met at residency of the Rev. L.H. Pedersen – for a reunion.

6-27-17 32 members of the Alpine club reached the top of A.B. Mountain . . . including L.H. Pedersen.

LOUIS AND FANNY

6-28-17 Women to aid plans for 4th of July. Mrs. L.H. Pedersen put on committee.

6-25-17 Chilkoot Campfire Girls Club Formed . . . Ruth Pedersen.

6-28-17 (Editorial) We are pleased to announce that Mr. Ralph Pedersen has accepted the position of editor of the Daily Alaskan and has taken hold of his new responsibilities with characteristic energy and thoroughness. Mr. Pedersen is no stranger to Skagway or Alaska, having made his home in Alaska for 14 years with the exception of the winter months, during which he was pursuing his studies at the University of Washington in Seattle. Prior to coming to Skagway he was located at Seward and Douglas and is therefore a real Alaskan in every sense of the word. While at the University Mr. Pedersen prepared himself for the duties, which he has now assumed, having taken the special course in journalism. Aside from being a natural writer he has had considerable experience in the mechanical production of a newspaper, having been employed in the printing departments of several newspapers ion the towns in which he has resided. We feel sure Mr. Pedersen will throw himself unreservedly into the editorial work of the Alaskan and we bespeak for him the hearty cooperation of our readers. L.S. Keller – Publisher. Personals. Mrs. J. M. Olsen will return to her home in Astoria on the Sophia, sailing Monday night.

7-30-17 (Editorial on Bert Howdeshall, a former editor of the Daily Alaskan, presumably written by Ralph Pedersen.)

8-1-17 Local Church to Call Pastor. At a meeting at 8 o'clock tonight a formal call will be issued to a pastor. Since the start of the Presbyterian Church last October Rev. L.H. Pedersen has continued at the unanimous request of the members. Now is the time to cement the relationship and place the church on a firmer foundation. Mr. Pedersen having signified his willingness to enter the Presbyterian Church and be received into the Presbytery of Alaska, the elders have called a meeting of the Congregation in order that financial arrangements may be perfected . . . (etc.)

8-3-17 German Spy Tells His Identity While Under Anesthesia (datelined Miami, Arizona, where Ralph M. Pedersen's first son, Richard Foote, was born 8 years later. Just an amazing coincidence as

DAN PEDERSEN

Miami, Ariz. was hardly known.)

8-7-17 Alpine Club to Go to Burrow Creek (those planning to go asked to leave their names at . . . Pedersen Bros and others)

8-11-17 The Reverend and Mrs. L.H. Pedersen made a quick trip this week to the top of A.B. Mountain. They left home in the morning and returned in the evening of the same day.

8-31-17 (Closed on Labor Day . . . Pedersen Bros.)

9-5-17 List of those who registered for the draft in Skagway – 81 total . . . Pedersen, Ralph M. Pedersen, Fred L.

9-18-17 Induction of the Rev. Mr. Pedersen. Presbytery of Alaska were meeting in Juneau. Recessed and will resume here – Skagway – on Wednesday and complete their business on Thursday. As the most important part will be the induction of the Rev. Mr. Pedersen as minister of the Skagway Presbyterian church the citizens would do well to embrace this opportunity of attending this service in token of their appreciation for the Rev. Mr. Pedersen, who has always stood for the best interests of the community, socially, morally and spiritually, since he came to the city 4 years ago. The Session.

9-26-17 Reports final session of Presbytery installing Rev. L.H. Pedersen as local pastor.

9-29-17 Reports on a packing box ("and a fine one") having been made by L.H. Pedersen for the Red Cross. Dinner given for minister and his wife by Mr. and Mrs. Ashe Stevens. . . . The Presbyterian Church entertained in honor of the Reverend L.H. Pedersen and Mrs. Pedersen and visiting members of the Presbytery at Pullen House on Tuesday. Beautiful flowers and autumn leaves. Wood fire in fireplace. Tables decorated with California poppies. Held in General Dining Room. Delicious dinner. Mr. Ralph M. Pedersen present. (Query: Why not Rev. Fred Pedersen?)

10-4-17 Average number of papers sold previous year "about 825"

10-6-17 Editor takes short trip. Ralph Pedersen, who for the past several months has held down the editor's desk of this paper, will be a passenger south on the Prince John for Seattle tonight, where he will undergo a physical examination by a specialist. Mr. Pedersen has taken hold of his work in a thorough manner, and has made good, making many friends for the Alaskan as well as creating some good business. He will be gone from his duties about 20 days, and while away will visit relatives in Seattle and Tacoma, and will call on his Alma Mater, the University of Washington, where he will mingle with old classmates. Week in Society: Ralph M. Pedersen, editor of the Skagway Daily Alaskan, will be a passenger south on the Prince John to Seattle. During Mr. Pedersen's absence, J.M. Keller will fill the editor's chair . . . .. Town Council equalized evaluation of personal property for taxation purposes. Pedersen &* Co. $221 to $421.

10-8-17 Personals. Ralph Pedersen (and others) took passage on the John for Seattle.

10-11-17 Letter to Ralph M. Pedersen, Editor, re his Sept. 20 letter. Reference donation of cast-off shoes . . . we would particularly thank you for the personal interest taken by you and your paper. New York Life Insurance Co., Seattle Branch. Shoes to go to France.

10-20-17 Oct. 24 to be national holiday, featuring Second Library Loan. Closing . . . Pedersen & Co.

10-25-17 $30,000 in liberty bonds bought. Qualified to serve . . . 37 Ralph Martin Pedersen, 55 Frederick Louis Pedersen (of 91) re draft.

10-26-17 Week in Society. Ralph M. Pedersen is home from a trip to Seattle. Mr. Pedersen reports a pleasant visit and a good voyage up on the Princess Alice. Mr. Pedersen is again in his place as the editor of the Skagway Daily Alaskan.

10-27-17 (Adv. Eight Weeks Till Christmas) . . . Why not make this a photographic Christmas? Portraits make Christmas Gifts that are individual, pleasing and useful. Reasonable in price. Your money will go further. "There's a photographer in your town." Albums, Hand Colored Enlargements, Postcards, Transparencies, Calendars, Picture Frames in stock sizes, Ripple Boards, Blotting Paper, Linen and Manila Envelopes, Calendar Pads, etc. The Pedersen Co., Inc. "The Christmas Store" (ads continue into 1918 with frequent changes of text)

11-17-18 Bolsheviski Forces in Control (but later issues report continuing strife in Russia, and Lenin not pictured as into clear power until well into 1918) Report on 4 coastal shipping and passenger boats damaged in previous month.

11-28-17 Food Savings Committee. Mrs. Fred L. Pedersen was unanimously elected Secretary (of a central committee). Skagway Offers Variety of Christmas Shoppers . . . at the Pedersen Co., a specialty is being made of portraits for Christmas. Beautiful hand colored photographs of Alaskan scenes and hand made Christmas greeting cards are on sale. Everything in the photo line and many novelties are offered to the Christmas trade.

12-19-17 A special meeting of Camp Skagway No. 1 of the Alaskan Brotherhood was held last night at which much business was contracted. Ralph M. Pedersen was initiated. (Special New Years edition of paper is announced)

12-20-17 (Punchy editorial written to encourage people to not only do their own business but to help the town generally) – typical of what Ralph might have been expected to write. Large ad also appeared from the paper itself – repeated for about a week – complaining against an unnamed business for taking its printing elsewhere when the Alaskan could have done it. Implicit that other business that could have been done in Skagway also taken elsewhere.

12-24-17 We wish you a Merry Christmas. The Pedersen Co. PS: No, we're not froze up.

12-26-17 Most severe weather on record, 25-30 degrees below zero yesterday.

12-29-17 The Week in Society. The Reverend and Mrs. L.H. Pedersen gathered all their Skagway relatives under their roof on Christmas Day for a family reunion. There were present Mrs. Captain Olsen, mother of Mr. Pedersen, Mr. and Mrs. Fred Pedersen, Mr. Ralph Pedersen, Miss Ruth Pedersen, Mr. Joseph Pedersen, and Willard and Andrew Pedersen. The day was happily spent and a fine dinner was served.

12-31-1917 Long editorial about Daily Alaskan. Started Feb. 1989 by

C.W. Dunbar. Taken over by L.S. Keller in 1907 after several other owners. Numerous other newspapers were established in Skagway but "The Alaskan was always looked upon as the exponent of the city's heights." Distributed over Yukon Basin, Whitehorse, Atlin, White Pass, Haines and Fort Seward, and sent to several states in north and Midwest. Covers flowers, gardens, Skagway as a home city, hikes, etc.

1-1-18 Extensive articles about business, etc. Many ads. Article on Skagway generally. Started in 1897. Now has population of about 1,000. Thumbnail sketches of Skagway businessmen. L.H. Pedersen, minister in the First Presbyterian Church, first came to Alaska in 1903, going direct to Douglas from Oregon. He served there for two years as missionary for the Methodist Church. His next move was to Seward in its boom days, where as Methodist minister he constructed a church and parsonage, and installed a YMCA in the city. In 1913 Rev. Mr. Pedersen came to Skagway where he served for four years in the Methodist work, and early this fall at the request of Skagway people and the consent of the two denominations, the Methodist work was turned over to the Presbyterians and he was called to be their minister. Besides church work, the Rev. Pedersen has been active in all civic works of this city. Frederick L. Pedersen, manager of the photographic firm of The Pedersen Co., came to Skagway first in 1914 and during the three months of the summer worked as a partner in the former firm of Pedersen Bros. The next summer he returned from his work at the University of Washington and earned enough money from the Pedersen Bros photo firm to put him through his final year in college. He is now manager of The Pedersen Co., an outgrowth of the former business, and intends to go east to Drew Seminary where he will prepare himself for the ministry. (Large two-column ad re The Pedersen Company, successor to Pedersen Brothers. We have more than 300 Alaskan negatives and manufacture Pedersen's Alaska Postcards and hand colored photo enlargements – known everywhere – considerable other text.)

1-31-18 16 soldiers arrived yesterday to guard city. (Apparently there was a general German plot expected around the US on Jan. 21 and the soldiers were sent up for that. Seemed to be expected to stay only a week or so.)

1-21-18 Editorial says there are fanatics even in Skagway who might destroy life and property. Urges people to stay calm. Retain morale. Says Skagway has a Council of Defense (and it is here to which suspicious acts are to be reported). Report on a speech by L.H. Pedersen: We are at war. He said three things are necessary to do. First we must have soldiers. Second we must have supplies. Third, we need means to purchase these supplies. Thus spoke L.H. Pedersen of the Skagway Four Minute Men to an audience in the Popular Picture Palace, Saturday night.

1-25-18 Announces appointment of a committee – Alpine Club: of Fred Pedersen . . . to work up the entertainment. Miss Agnes Moffatt and Ralph M. Pedersen appointed to secure the necessary room.

1-30-18 Rev. L.H. Pedersen has been appointed Skagway member of the Committee on Civilian Relief (Home Service) . . . to assist wives and families of soldiers and sailors.

2-18-18 Under direction of Fred Pedersen . . . following skit was given at Alpine Club Friday . . . Jack Frost. Fred Pedersen. Human pipe organ was played by Mrs. Fred Pedersen.

2-19-18 Draft numbers. Frederic Louis Pedersen 48. Ralph Martin Pedersen 64 (of 91) but will actually be called up by classes.

2-23-18 Ralph Pedersen, editor of the Skagway Daily Alaskan, went to Fort William H. Seward on Saturday last on business and was detained for a day or two, as there was no boat. Mr. Pedersen made the trip up in a small gas launch that he might not be absent from his post of duty.

2-26-18 Contains large ad by Keller Bros Drugs for inexpensive Kodak cameras. Thereafter frequently repeated. (Fred Pedersen had also been selling cameras)

3-18-18 The Pedersen Company received their first wholesale tourist order to postal cards of Alaska last week, three weeks in advance of any other season. This may be taken as an indication of expected tourist travel to Alaska.

3-19-18 Important meeting of Skagway Alpine Club tonight. Miss

LOUIS AND FANNY

Ruth Pedersen will render a selection on the piano.

3-29-18. Enthusiastic meeting of Alpine Club. Newly elected officers: Vice President Fred L. Pedersen. Librarian and Historian, Mrs. F.L. Pedersen. Three members at large . . . L.H. Pedersen. Ruth Pedersen played the opening number.

3-22-18 On Thursday a delightful family gathering took place in the Manse the occasion being the birthday of Ruth, daughter of the Rev. and Mrs. L.H. Pedersen. No one was present except the relatives and Miss Frances Kennedy, a close friend of Miss Pedersen, Mrs. Andrew Stevenson and her little daughter. Ruth contributed to the feast of good things by baking a fine birthday cake handsomely decorated with an appropriate inscription and candles. Along with the cake was given a goodly sized freezer of ice cream. This is the sixteenth birthday of Miss Ruth Pedersen and all her many friends are wishing her sixteen year measures of happiness.

4-13-18 Rev. Pedersen received a night letter this morning from his son Ralph, in which Ralph states that he has accepted a position with the YMCA and his duties will take him all over Washington. (Duties not stated in the cablegram)

5-18-18 Shaping Plans for Big Red Cross Fund Drive. Rev. L.H. Pedersen: Duty of everyone to do our bit. In favor of move for regular monthly contributions. Willing and ready to do his part.

6-1-18 On Tuesday, the Reverend L.H. Pedersen, Mrs. Pedersen and their young daughter, Miss Ruth went to Haines. Mr. Pedersen returned the same day, while Mrs. Pedersen and her daughter will remain for a rest of a few weeks.

6-22-18 Mrs. L.H. Pedersen, Miss Ruth Pedersen, Willard Pedersen and Andrew Pedersen are home from a vacation in Haines. Miss Ruth Pedersen has regained her health and is glad to be at home again.

6-25-18 Alpine Club schedules. Tues July 9, top of A.B. Mountain. Guide Rev. L.H. Pedersen . . . Decided to make a photo record. Turned over: to Mrs. Fred Pedersen with power to secure the necessary photographs and a suitable album which was to be of substantial make . . .

6-29-18 Editorial: Starting Mon July 1 the Skagway Daily Alaskan will be somewhat different on Monday, Wednesday and Friday. On those days there will be a one-page news bulletin with full cable press reports and the most important local news. Tuesday, Thursday and Saturday will continue to be 4 pages. The editorial noted there had been a daily deficit for some time. N.B. One page meant one sheet on both sides.

7-6-18 Repeats a Whitehorse Star editorial saying why the Daily Alaskan held so tenaciously to a daily newspaper was hard to say. . . . "There is about as much need for a daily issue of a paper in that town as there is in Whitehorse, and that is none."

7-15-18 Rev. and Mrs. L.H. Pedersen went to Denver glacier this morning. They are escorting a party of tourists who will spend the day there. Mr. Pedersen says the trail is in very good shape this year and that if a couple of days work was done in the way of cutting the high grass and trimming out some of the branches that overhang the path it would make a good trail, and many would take advantage of the fine weather to go out to the glacier. It is up to the Commercial Club to look into this matter.

7-20-18 Article reporting the start of a daily paper in Cordova, the Cordova Daily Herald . . .. The Reverend LH. Pedersen will move his family to Tacoma the latter part of August and will devote a year to manual labor, taking a rest from his chosen work as minister. A skilled mechanic, Mr. Pedersen will find profitable work in Tacoma. Joseph Pedersen, son of the Reverend and Mrs. L.H. Pedersen, writes that he is doing fine in the shipyards of Tacoma. Joe is earning a very excellent wage and when his apprenticeship is completed his salary will be much increased. Joseph is making good in his work as he has always done and that means success through life . . . .. On Wednesday, Captain Barrett of China, master of river boats of that country for twenty years, the Reverend Mr. Dennett of New York city, Miss Finner of California, Miss Yeats and Miss Lee of Regina, were distinguished guests at dinner in the home of Rev. and Mrs. L.H. Pedersen. On Monday Mr. and Mrs. Pedersen acted as trail guides for their guests on a trip to Denver Glacier. Miss Elain Stowers was also a guest to the glacier . . . . A letter from Joseph Pedersen . . . to his home was given a reporter for the Daily Alaskan. The letter is very interesting but of too intimate and personal a nature to permit of printing entire. Mr. Pedersen has met and visited with nearly all the people who have left Skagway recently and he reports them all well and profitably employed. Among the number are the Friedenthal family and the Huntleys, Mrs. James Collison and her family, Emerson Rogers, Arthur McKay and others. Joseph is still in the shipyards at Tacoma and is almost through with his apprenticeship and then he will go to Auburn as a "regular" and receive a much better wage -- $6.00 per day. He is very well and very happy in his new work which he likes much better than the work he was in Seattle – that of airship building.

7-27-18 Mr. and Mrs. Fred Pedersen . . . (others) were dinner guests of Mr. and Mrs. L.A. Harrison on Sunday night. Skagway Alpine Club Excursion to Lake Bennett for Local Red Cross Chapter. 138 persons took advantage of the low fare to again visit this historic spot (through British Columbia to the Fort Seward area). Rev. L.H. Pedersen was there with his ever-attractive suggestions . . .

8-8-18 Joseph Pedersen Writes Home. Joseph Pedersen, in an interesting letter to a friend in Skagway, writes: "Well, how is Skagway? I hope it is still on the map. I don't care if it isn't. They cannot take it off the earth, so I'm going back someday just because it's Skagway. I suppose you would like to know what I'm doing. I'm just building ships. It's my old trade. I began when I was old enough to handle a jack knife and run away from home. These boats are built on the same lines as the Pal Pyra, have five masts and a bow sprit, double funnels, double engines, double boilers, twin screws. They are both steam and sail, have electric lights and wireless, two anti-submarine guns, one forward and one aft. Every chest in the yard (4,000 of them) swells with pride as one goes steaming past and they all give three cheers and the vessel answers with three toots. The vessels all go to the French government. When they leave the skids they fly the French flag on the stern and the American flag on the bow. They slide in stern first. As soon as one vessel leaves the skid the keel is laid for the next. They cannot afford to wait ten minutes. We have already launched eight boats and will soon launch another.

8-10-18 Mrs. Fred L. Falconer, wife of the resident Presbyterian clergyman of Kinkwan, was a guest of the Reverend and Mrs. L.H. Pedersen on Tuesday. Mrs. Falconer was in town to make arrangements for her oldest daughter's entrance into the high school of Skagway.

8-12-18 Where Are the Skagway Home Guards? . . . Mrs. L.H. Pedersen was given a delightful reception on Friday evening in the Ziskon bungalow in the South end (?) by the leaders of the WCTU. Mrs. Pedersen has been for years connected with the temperance work and has held many offices during her membership and this social affair was in honor of Mrs. Pedersen's good work and to bid her goodbye and success in her new home in Nevada, where she and her family will go at the end of the present month. (Has been territorial treasurer for the last 3 years. Given beautiful leather bound volume of the life of Frances T. Willard. Beautiful flowers and dinner.)

8-17-18 Large party scaled Denver Glacier under the guidance of Rev. L.H. Pedersen, taking the regular White Pass train Thursday. They had an avalanche-like thrill on the trip.

8-22-18 Skagway will be nearly deserted this winter, says the Juneau Dispatch.

8-23-18 Farewell Reception for Rev. Pedersen and Family. A farewell reception will be tendered Rev. L.H. Pedersen and family at the Presbyterian Church next Tuesday evening at 8 o'clock. The general public is cordially invited to attend the reception and our especial invitation is extended to the members of the various organizations with which Rev. Pedersen or members of his family were associated to be present. A program will be given under the direction of Mr. and Mrs. W.C. Blanchard, which will include instrumental and vocal subjects and some readings. Refreshments will be served during the evening. Rev. Pedersen and family will leave on the Prince Rupert on Saturday, August 31, and after spending a few weeks with friends in Seattle and Tacoma, proceed to someplace in Nevada where they will remain for some time to come. Nevada has been selected as a place of residence owing to the damp climate along the coast, and it is deemed more helpful to various members of the family.

LOUIS AND FANNY

8-31-18 The reception given the Reverend L.H. Pedersen and his family in the Presbyterian church on Tuesday was a delightful and harmonious gathering together of friends of the departing family. Nothing was spared to make this a long to be remembered farewell. The church was a bower of beauty. Beautiful cut flowers, ferns and potted plants filled the front of the church and window ledges. The Altar, chancel organ and piano were tastefully and profusely decked with flowers of many colors and harmoniously blending. The committee on decoration may be proud of their success. A well-rendered program under the supervision of Mr. and Mrs. W.C. Blanchard was a delightful feature of the evening. Everyone did his or her part well, and the repeated applause showed the appreciation of the audience. The presentation speeches and responses were well done and full of deep feeling. The Reverend Mr. Pedersen and Mrs. Pedersen were given a purse of gold; Mr. and Mrs. Fred L. Pedersen were the recipients of a very handsome percolator, and Miss Ruth Pedersen, former superintendent of the Cradle Role in the Presbyterian Sunday School, was given a beautifully carved and stained ivory pen holder and a pretty gold locket filled with gold nuggets. A most delightful luncheon of many kinds of cake and excellent coffee was served by the ladies of the church. Our good friends "the Pedersens" will leave on Monday on the Princess Sophia for Seattle, and then proceed to their destination by rail.

N.B. The Princess Sophia sank in a storm in October off the Alaskan coast taking many lives.

Acknowledgments

A book like this really is a collaborative project. The story has been pulled together at different times over much of the last century by various family members who tackled different pieces of it in different ways. This book is the beneficiary of many people's efforts, some of whom I name here, with apologies to those I fail to acknowledge.

Frederick L. Pedersen

Louis and Fanny's oldest son, Frederick L. Pedersen, awakened my interest in family history in 1964 when he gave me a family heirloom, a trunk built by his father's father in 1867 for the son he would never live to see. A yellowed card inside the trunk's lid explains:

This trunk was made in 1867 in Tromsoe, Norway, by Klaus Pedersen for his son (yet unborn) Louis H Pedersen. Repaired and tray added by said son in 1938 in Bellingham, Washington. The original nails used were made by hand. (Signed) Louis H. Pedersen

That humble trunk must have been an immense comfort to my grandfather. It was all he ever had of his dad.

Joseph Turner Pedersen

In 1968, shortly after my dad retired from teaching, he devoted an entire year to researching family history. The outcome was a family tree going back to the 1700s on his father's side, along with a comprehensive narrative about our family that remains the definitive source document. Dad died in 1992.

Cora Turner Wahlstrom

In 1992 I obtained a wealth of source material about my grandmother Fanny's side of the family in the documents my great aunt Cora passed along to Dad to help in his research. Included were the Turner family Bible and a collection of obituaries, marriage licenses and other papers Cora had preserved. Cora lived on Camano Island, not far from my parents' home in Mount Vernon, and we visited her often on trips to our family's getaway cabin. Cora died of a head injury in 1973 or 74, sustained in a Christmas Eve fall in our home. I still remember her quick wit and intellect, important clues to the personality of my own grandmother.

Martha Eloise Turner Murfin

Martha Murfin, my grandmother's niece, held the keys to a huge piece of Fanny's story, including a whole box of letters her father wrote as a Union soldier in the Civil War. A few years before Martha's death in 2007 she turned over this trove from her attic to her nephew, Michael Coffey. Martha was beloved in her community of Long Beach, Washington, as both a journalist and friend of children and families who needed a hand.

Michael Coffey

My cousin Michael Coffey of Seattle and I worked intensively as a family research team for about two years, exchanging many emails a day. Michael was the right person for Martha to trust with the Turner archives because he's a diligent student of both genealogy and history, committed to accuracy and the best tools of technology. Together, we found relatives no one knew existed, and pieced together details of the family story long lost from memory.

Many others also supplied crucial pieces of the story. The danger of naming any is of missing many others, but I must mention especially Uncle Willard's wife, **Helen Hunter Pedersen**; my brothers **Fred** and **Joe**, my sister **Frances**; and my cousin **Richard F. Pedersen**.

DAN PEDERSEN

ABOUT THE AUTHOR

Dan Pedersen is a native of Western Washington. He received two journalism degrees from the University of Washington in the turbulent 1960s and 70s, served in the US Air Force and went on to become a reporter and editor for several newspapers in Idaho and Washington, including a large outdoor weekly.

He writes a weekly blog about nature and small-town life, and is the author of these books:

Final Deception: A Whidbey Island Mystery (Amazon)
Outdoorsy Male: Short Stories and Essays (Amazon)
My Whidbey: Exploring an Island With Fresh Eyes (Blurb Books)
Trails Through Time: Turners and Pedersens (Blurb Books)

Printed in Great Britain
by Amazon

70548473R00119